'I recommend Robin's book
to hear. His writings are full
unusual ability to help us un~
light of the revealed Christ.'
Roy Godwin, Director the Ffald-y-Brenin Trust, and author of The Grace
Outpouring

'This is an important book on a subject which is often stressed
but rarely discussed in detail. I particularly treasure and was
moved by the central section – which takes up more than a third
of the book – in which he speaks about the important role of
silences. In introducing us to the fear and language of silence he
reminds the reader to "listen to its sound, tone and texture,
inflections and nuances, to observe the levels and stages of
silence, and above all the therapist needs to listen to his own
experience of silence, and try to sense how the client is
experiencing it". He then goes on to give us "as start" a
classification of 12 types of positive, negative, neutral silences. It
is a useful guide, making us aware of the extensive range of types
of silences and encouraging us to develop as fine an ear as we can,
in order to have a better attunement to our client's/patient's
feelings. This chapter, like the rest of the book, contains many
wonderful quotations, ranging from the Bible to philosophers,
poets and writers through the ages. '
*Isca Wittenberg, Consultant Psychotherapist and past Vice-Chairman,
Tavistock Clinic, London; author of* Psychoanalytic Insight and
Relationships: A Kleinian Approach

'In *Listening* Daniels succeeds magnificently not just in describing
but actually creating the very "climate" and "atmosphere" of
which he speaks so wisely. This little volume is a masterclass in
what helps and what hinders this holy art and a welcome resource
for anyone involved in accompaniment. For me, reading these
pages was itself therapeutic – and a sheer delight!'
Canon John Udris, Spiritual Director, St Mary's College, Oscott

'This book extends seamlessly from Robin Daniels' wealth of
people helping experience and love of music. While primarily

focused on the therapist and client relationship, the book offers many thought-provoking and accessible riches for pastoral helpers of all kinds. With remarkable wisdom, spiritual insight and literary skill, Robin melodically identifies the essential components, as well as subtle pitfalls, involved in listening to others and guiding them through their healing and growth.

'For therapists the familiar is presented with articulate freshness. For pastoral carers, spiritual directors and clergy the helping process is unravelled in a way which can imaginatively be transposed. For both groupings, the book in its meticulous concern, reminds us of the great privilege of serving others with selfless and humble attitude, recognising that both helper and listener are learners together. It is a work composed intelligently from the heart for the heart with passionate intent to tune our ears to the harmonious and discordant within ourselves and those we seek to help.'

Teresa Onions, Former Director of Pastoral Care UK

'When God said to Solomon, "Ask whatever you want," Solomon asked for "a heart that listens". Robin Daniels encourages us also to find within ourselves a heart that listens. This is a courageous book written by a courageous therapist, firmly rooted in his own quiet relationship with God, and speaking out from within this context. He talks movingly about the mutual growth, spiritual, emotional and thoughtful, involved for both speaker and listener when engaged in the activity of being totally present to each other, in the present moment. He gives us the confidence to be silent, to be in communion with the other and trust the unconscious unfolding growth that is possible when we let go of the control of busying ourselves with being in charge of change. A wonderful and enlightening book for everyone.'

Hermione Roff, Systemic Child and Family Therapist; Author of Reflective Interpersonal Therapy for Children and Parents

'In this luminous book, Robin Daniels invites us both to draw close to the heart of God and to accompany others on that journey. For Robin, being listened to is the key to our healing and to that journey. Those who seek to listen to others will find here many encouragements and helps for this challenging and often complex work. Robin quotes Einstein's dictum that an inner world does not come without a struggle. Many readers of this book will find themselves better equipped for that struggle and feel a deep sense of gratitude to Robin for this legacy.'

Mark Bryant, Anglican Bishop of Jarrow and Suffragan Bishop of Durham

'Listen to the author of this book, because he has words shaped by hard-won wisdom. Savour the insights and experience which inform each paragraph, because they will stop you in your tracks and lead you to rethink your own professional practice and your own personal relating. Don't anticipate a 'learned treatise', but draw on the rich resources which support the author's reflections. Sit with Robin Daniels and be touched by his analytically-honed perception, his deep and inclusive Christian faith, and his generosity of heart and mind.'

Fr Brendan Callaghan SJ, sometime Senior Lecturer in the Psychology of Religion in the University of London, Principal of Heythrop College, Master of Campion Hall Oxford

Robin takes us with him on an adventure journey into the world of listening. His book is a clearly-written exposition of the art of listening, and affords a valuable insight into the world of psychotherapy. Robin's many and varied quotations are an added bonus, as are his references to music. I would recommend the book to anyone who is searching for truth and wholeness in their lives.

Sister Benedict Brown, Benedictine nun and sub-prioress at Turvey Abbey, Bedfordshire

LISTENING

HEARING THE HEART

ROBIN DANIELS

instant
apostle

First published in Great Britain by Instant Apostle, 2017

Instant Apostle
The Barn
1 Watford House Lane
Watford
Herts
WD17 1BJ

Unless otherwise stated, Scripture quotations are from the Revised Standard Version of the Bible, copyright © 1946, 1952, and 1971 National Council of the Churches of Christ in the United States of America. Used by permission. All rights reserved.

Scripture quotations marked KJV are taken from The Authorized (King James) Version. Rights in the Authorized Version in the United Kingdom are vested in the Crown. Reproduced by permission of the Crown's patentee, Cambridge University Press.

Every effort has been made to seek permission to use copyright material reproduced in this book. The publisher and author apologise for those cases where permission might not have been sought and, if notified, will formally seek permission at the earliest opportunity.

The views and opinions expressed in this work are those of the author and do not necessarily reflect the views and opinions of the publisher.

British Library Cataloguing-in-Publication Data

A catalogue record for this book is available from the British Library

This book and all other Instant Apostle books are available from Instant Apostle:

Website: www.instantapostle.com

E-mail: info@instantapostle.com

ISBN 978-1-909728-74-5

Printed in Great Britain

Contents

Foreword

Listening is primarily intended for members of the caring professions. It is, however, much more than a standard account of its subject. It plumbs deeper layers of life, has a wider vision and radiates humanity.

The book concerns the fundamental ingredients of a therapeutic alliance. It sets out the elements and ethos of a healing rapport and relationship – structured, yes, but free of strictures.

The book is full of essential understanding about the nature and practice of therapy, and about healthy, wholesome living.

Moreover, the author explores features of therapy which are taken for granted or on trust and often not overtly acknowledged. He bravely explores areas – such as the fear and use of silence – which are elusive, but vital and full of treasure.

These are not scientific pursuits, and they cannot be reduced to formulae or techniques, for, as Robin Daniels emphasises and reminds us, the understanding of two-way communication is an art form and, as such, a lifelong development.

We tend to reach for labels rather than seek insight into the connection and complementarity between inner and outer, and between order and chaos. The author has avoided that trap, for which he is to be commended.

This book contains vital, poignant links between current sociological features and their effect on all forms of life. We reap whatever we sow, but the soil and the climate govern and determine the harvest.

The art of therapy is timing. Robin Daniels forges original links between time and timing as experienced in therapy, in music and in journeys (inner and outer), drawing on his considerable experience in these three fields.

His sources and references are impressive. They demonstrate the range of his richly cultured personality, and his admirable (because non-pontifical) erudition, whetting this reader's appetite for more of his wisdom and his humanity.

Eva A. Seligman, former Psychotherapist at the Tavistock Institute of Marital Studies, and Training Analyst of the Society of Analytical Psychology; author of The Half-Alive Ones

Notes on the author, by his widow

When a person dies we have the chance to see the themes of their life in the round. When we are caught up in the midst of life, it can seem like the back of a tapestry: a jumble of colours, knots and stray threads, and no sign of any coherent picture. It is said that at the end of a person's life the tapestry is turned around, and what appeared to be disparate colours and threads reveal a picture of intricate beauty.

Listening in the professional and personal life

If I were to summarise the central theme to emerge from the different threads of Robin's professional life, and a key feature of his personal relationships, it would be listening. He studied music with Alan Rowlands and was a music critic with *The Croydon Times*. He was a writer, and three of his early books were based on interviews: *Conversations with Cardus*, *Conversations with Menuhin* and *Conversations with Coggan*.[1] These all involved listening to and eliciting the wisdom and experience of the other – always seeking to draw out the best, not delve in the shadows.

Robin's voluntary work for various churches took the form of listening: listening to couples, marriage enrichment, group work, visiting the blind, a reflecting group for hospital

---

[1] Robin's books were: *Conversations with Coggan* (Hodder, 1983); *Conversations with Menuhin* (Time-Warner, 1979); *Conversations with Cardus* (Gollancz, 1976); *Blackpool Football: The Official Club History* (Robert Hale, 1972); and *Cardus: Celebrant of Beauty* (Palatine Books, 2009).

chaplains, and interviewing his heroes and mentors. Lastly, his main profession was that of a psychotherapist, which involved depth listening to the soul-searching of individuals and couples in various forms of distress.

In his personal life Robin would tend to listen to the other person and draw them out. He didn't usually volunteer his opinions or share his personal experiences. This stemmed partly from being of a private temperament and partly from a deep inner and spiritual life which meant that the hinterland he inhabited was intrinsically private. He was aware of the potential for sharing of spiritual and internal things to lead to pride. These trends were reinforced by professional training and practice which eschewed personal disclosure on the part of the therapist.

Robin was not self-preoccupied, so he did not have to prove himself by sharing his opinions. He was relatively 'up to date' and trusted in his own equipment and God's guidance, so he did not need to offload on to or seek advice from others. His approach had the effect of eliciting and encouraging the wisdom of the other. As one friend put it, 'When you were having a conversation with Robin, he made you feel like you were the star player.'

It may be that listening was a sort of personal asceticism. Robin occasionally spoke of how one might become aware of something in a client months before the client becomes aware of it, but would have to restrain from intervening, in order for the client to arrive at the insight or discovery for themselves. Self-discovered insights always yield more fruit.

There was a degree of loneliness that came with Robin's acute sensitivity and discernment. These gifts meant he could see things that others did not see and had intuitions he wished to heed, but which flew in the face of the way the world saw things, and of the pragmatic approach.

It is not for nothing that Robin's gravestone bears the words, 'Robin Listened'. In reading this book, it is not that you will necessarily find things that have not been said elsewhere –

although I do believe there is an originality to Robin's philosophy and practice – but more that you will be learning the art of listening from a man who really did practise it. Words which have been truly lived are more likely to bear fruit in the reader's life.

I once asked Robin how he listened in his professional practice, and how he knew what to say. He said he tried to listen simultaneously to God, to his own instincts and feelings, and to the other person, and was then guided in the moment.

Music

Robin was initiated into the art of listening by his American grandmother, a Dutch immigrant, Elsa Holch. She would 'take them to a concert' (turn on the radio), give Robin a 'programme' (a magazine), and then model to the young boy turning a key over the lips in order to open the ears to listen.

This love of music remained with Robin throughout his life. He was especially fond of the compositions of Handel, Beethoven and Mozart, and disliked dissonant music. When Robin was 14, he and a friend wrote to Pope St John XXIII suggesting that Mozart should be canonised. This love of music translated itself into the metaphors Robin used in the consulting room: references to 'chromatic notes', the presence of 'vibrato' in a person's communications, and his description of himself as an 'adagio man'.

He described his ear as his instrument. Robin believed that listening to music was an education in all forms of human listening. It is fitting therefore that the final section of this book should be a monograph on Beethoven, which ends with an invitation to listen together to Nathan Milstein playing the composer's Violin Concerto with the Pittsburg Symphony Orchestra, conducted by Steinberg. The reader is encouraged to purchase or download the material from EMI Classics before they reach the end of the book.

Chastity of the ear

We are familiar with the three monkeys covering their eyes, ears and mouth: 'See no evil, hear no evil, speak no evil'. Robin believed in preserving the 'chastity of the ear'. This referred partly to shielding oneself from hearing discordant material (except in the consulting room): gossip, or news of unpleasant or violent events. He was a walking example of the man described in Isaiah 33:15 who 'stops his ears from hearing of bloodshed and shuts his eyes from looking on evil'. This translated itself to turning off the television if something jarring came on, and nimbleness in turning the course of conversation to lines which were more edifying to speaker and listener.

'Chastity of the ear' also referred to a certain abstinence when it came to listening to musical works of real heroism and stature. He had a 'Restricted list', on which appeared the following works: Beethoven's Symphonies 4 and 5; Beethoven's Violin Concerto; Beethoven's Fifth Piano Concerto (The Emperor); and Brahms' Violin Concerto. Robin believed these works should only be listened to occasionally and then only ever with full attention (never as background music), so that an attitude of first-time listening could be preserved. The related theme of 'first-time seeing' is explored in his book *The Virgin Eye: Towards a Contemplative View of Life*.[2]

Professional influences

It was while working as a fundraiser for the charity Scope and coming into contact with people with cerebral palsy that Robin first became aware of a vocation to the caring professions. He trained as a counsellor at the Westminster Pastoral Foundation (WPF), which was then trailblazing a collaboration between the healing ministries of the church and the world of therapy. At WPF his supervisor was David Holt, a Jungian analyst who had

---

[2] Instant Apostle, 2016.

trained at the C. G. Jung Institute in Zurich, who was a huge inspiration and influence.

Robin subsequently qualified as a social worker (doing particular studies on Child Guidance clinics and Women's Refuge centres). He then did his analytic training at the Lincoln Clinic – a course which was primarily Freudian. However, the key elements which influence a psychotherapist's style are the supervision and personal analysis one receives, which in Robin's case were both conducted by Jungians (trained with the Society of Analytical Psychology).

His Christian faith also shaped his work and, although he did not proselytise in the consulting room, it added to the depth he could bring if a client brought their own faith into the room. He didn't use a couch, and tended to see clients once or twice a week, as contracted.

Dreams

This background gave Robin a deep respect for the wisdom of the psyche, for the need to listen to and trust it, and a belief in its propensity to self-heal. He thought that doubts, instincts, intuitions and symbols in daily life should be taken seriously.

He had a great respect for the importance of dreams. Following Freud, he divided these into four main types: filing/processing-type dreams (where the psyche is essentially using the time of sleep to get up to date; 'wish fulfilment' dreams containing longings that are not fulfilled in the outer life; dreams about past events (often traumatic) that encourage the psyche to do more work on the issue; and lastly intuitive/guidance-type dreams (prophetic dreams being very rare and falling into this last category).

Robin would encourage others to 'free associate'[3] with the subject matter of the dream; to look at how the dream felt; to consider, 'Why did this dream come now?' and to look for other dreams of the same night (and the order) or those in a series over several nights. He eschewed pat interpretations, seeing the meaning of a dream as individual and unique to the dreamer.

Levels of sharing

Robin had a helpful summary of different levels of sharing (as to depth of intimacy):

1. Talking about things outside the room and outside ourselves

2. Less personal things about me and what I have done (my interests)

3. More personal things about myself and my history

4. Things about you and me ('us')

These are helpful guidelines for any kind of encounter. They also show why boundaries are so important in encounters where any deeper kind of sharing is likely to occur; indeed, where it is essential for the person's growth. In therapy or in spiritual direction, in pastoral care or confession, a person is likely to need to explore in the third category, and in forms of therapy where the transference is openly named and worked with, in category four. This will result in a depth of intimacy that can only be safely navigated where there are boundaries as to space, time, frequency, touch and personal disclosure (by the one in a predominantly listening mode).

---

[3] Free association means allowing oneself to spontaneously link to ideas, words, images and events suggested by the subject matter of the dream, without censoring or repressing them.

Clearly, therapeutic boundaries will not be appropriate in their entirety to all types of listening work – a priest, for instance, is not a psychotherapist – but there is much that those in ministry can learn from the world of therapy and appropriately adapt to their own settings. This book is also intended to be of benefit to anyone who is called to listen informally, which includes most of us. Clearly, the formal boundaries and neutrality of the therapist are not appropriate in such contexts, and readers will need to be selective about how they apply some of the recommendations that are particular to the consulting room.

Qualities of a listener

When I was considering training as a therapist, Robin suggested some qualities that he thought were essential in a therapist (and would apply to anyone with a listening ministry):

- Groundedness – leading a rounded life

- Respect for the client's pace of insight and growth, tiptoeing around sensitive areas and respecting defences

- Observation – as to own and patient's reactions and the transference

- Self-awareness and self-control (awareness of own vulnerable side and memories)

- Attentiveness – so as to remember details, to make links and be in the present moment, and to choose timing

- Empathy and compassion – warmth and concern for the client's preoccupations; wanting the best for him or her

- Intellect – to convey understanding of the person and what they share and to make sense of it

- Fascination with the work, with other people and capacity for lifelong self-growth

- Facility with language – clear and adapted to the individual, especially with regard to choosing imagery with which the other person will resonate

- Patience – so as to respect the client's pace, allowing time to reveal more

- Boundaries – communicated to the other person's conscious and unconscious – to enable clarity of expectations and enable one to give fully within these limits

- Good self-esteem

- Humility from a foundation of confidence: seeing that the work is done by 1) God; 2) the client; and 3) the listener (in that order)

- Acceptance that you may not see the fruits of your labour

- Easy and natural manner

- Reassuring manner and reliability, conveying confidence, liking and trust in the client and belief in the other's potential

- Conveying total permission to explore the shadow side

- Intuition

Time

I believe that the key feature of Robin's life that enabled him to listen at such depth was his slow pace. Robin inhabited time in a different way to most of us. Many of us can be caught on a sort of conveyor belt, moving through life at breakneck speed in a way that causes us to react rather than respond to events and people.

I met Robin on a day entitled 'The Poet's Eye' in which he was encouraging us to see life as the child, poet or artist does – with innocence, as if for the first time. He opened that day with the words, 'All time is God's time.' Robin was a good steward of time because he saw it not as his time but as God's. An encounter with Robin was one in which the sense of time as *chronos* (time which ticks) stepped aside for a *kairos* experience: a moment of time where eternity can break through.

The fullness of his personal and professional encounters was no doubt shaped by the traditional 50-minute hour – a boundary which at the same time as 'limiting' was the necessary precondition for depth meeting, intimate encounter, creative listening and sharing.

Savouring encounters was part of his attitude to time. Robin encouraged clients to arrive early for sessions and to carve out time after meetings to reflect, journal and savour. Through this practice (which he applied loosely to his own encounters), they were encouraged that they would benefit more from any meeting.

By restraining from providing answers or advice, and by encouraging those he walked alongside to tune into and respect their own needs, feelings, doubts and instincts, Robin enabled them to find the wisdom innate within themselves. By his confidence in the other person's equipment, he encouraged them to trust that they could find the answers for themselves by a deep listening to the promptings of God in prayer, to the symbols in the environment, to the so-called coincidences of life, and to instincts and feelings. The inspirations that come through these means, checked out with a wise other, and subject to any obligations of obedience to which we may be bound (including to the Word of God), could – he helped us believe – be trusted and held to even in the face of opposition and incomprehension by others.

Robin knew therapy was messy, not neat. He believed that though a person may feel they are pursuing random disparate lines of enquiry and going off on tangents, in the end the journey of therapy would – like a map of the London Underground – be seen to join up into something of coherence.

This is a bit like the threads on the tapestry of Robin's life – a life which knew suffering and rejection; a virtuous, well-ordered life which blended thanksgiving and praise, attention and listening, a slow pace and encouragement of others, and small acts done with love – to form a picture of great originality and fullness, which I, for one, am grateful to have shared in.

Katherine Daniels

LISTENING

Introduction

Every meeting is judgement, is crisis, is a situation in which we are called either to receive Christ, or to be Christ's messenger to the other person [or both]. If only we realized that the whole of life has this intensity of meaning.

Metropolitan Anthony[4]

The great Jewish philosopher Martin Buber wrote of an encounter he had with a young man who came to seek his counsel.

> What happened was no more than that one forenoon, after a morning of 'religious' enthusiasm, I had a visit from an unknown young man, without being there in spirit. I certainly did not fail to let the meeting be friendly, I did not treat him any more remissly than all his contemporaries who were in the habit of seeking me out about this time of day. ... I conversed attentively and openly with him – only I omitted to guess the questions which he did not put. Later, not long after, I learned from one of his friends – he himself was no longer alive – the essential content of these questions; I learned that he had

[4] Anthony Bloom, *School of Prayer* (London: Darton, Longman and Todd, 1993).

not come to me casually, but borne by destiny, not for a chat but for a decision. He had come to me, he had come in this hour. What do we expect when we are in despair and yet go to a man? Surely a presence by means of which we are told that nevertheless there is meaning.[5]

Buber later learned that this young man had died at the front in the First World War 'out of that kind of despair that may be partially defined as "no longer opposing one's own death"'. For Buber this encounter was 'an event of judgement' and marked a moment of personal conversion. He came to see that, following a morning spent in prayer, he had not been present to this young man: he had missed 'the question not spoken' – a question about trust in existence. It led him to fundamentally reorientate his approach to seeking God – no longer on the mountain peaks of mystical prayer – but in everyday encounter and dialogue with his neighbour.

One core feature of the art of listening is to listen with the inner ear as well as – perhaps more than – with the outer ear. Buber thought the man was just on a social visit. He had missed the underlying tone of a fateful mood, self-doubting and life-questioning. Sometimes in our work or daily encounters attentive and deep listening could make the difference between life and death. Even – sometimes especially – the once-only encounter can be life enhancingly precious.

Yet the nurturing, the fostering, of this most noble of human gifts – to listen: to receive, accept and affirm another person as he or she truly is – tends to rate low in education and teaching. Because sight is the most influential of the five senses, what we see tends to outrank what we hear.

Of the three main communication modes – speaking, listening and writing – listening is the most used. From early

[5] Maurice S. Friedman, *Martin Buber's Life and Work* (Wayne State University Press, 1988), p.188.

childhood we tune in for so many hours each week to the media, in its varied and proliferating forms, as well as listening to one another, person to person. As technology expands our communication options, so the depth of our communicating decreases.

I know of one supervisor who used to ask members of his team to reflect on their pastoral visits: 'You seem so preoccupied by what you said. Now please tell me what the other person said.' They had often forgotten.

Many children learn about listening only from being conditioned by absorbing, deep into the psyche, a series of orders:

- Shut up!

- Pay attention!

- Don't interrupt!

- I'm talking to you. Listen!

These orders, repeated day after day, often in a harsh, loud, negative or punishing tone, leave a deep impression on a child's psyche. Thus the gift of listening, human and humanising, comes to be seen as, at best, a faculty to be used grudgingly or unwillingly. Eloquence wins far more praise and prizes than its vitally necessary counterpart: the quieter qualities of patient, understanding, self-effacing listening.

Compounding these are other fundamental and personality-forming factors in Western and Westernised societies. The prevalence of the internet, online shopping and banking, mechanised supermarket tills, email and social media are replacing telephone and face-to-face interactions. Written or typed communications are now both instant and global.

The amount of time spent by people, of all ages, in front of the television, computer and other electronic devices limits time to listen to family members, and makes listening passive and often escapist rather than active and creative.

The ever-faster pace of life is the largest of the malign influences on person-to-person listening-skills. A person asks, 'How are you?' when steaming ahead, and the questioner frequently fails to stop and wait to hear a reply. I have been reflecting on the pace of life nowadays, since hearing a philologist say, 'How symbolic of our society that the phrase "up to scratch" is being displaced by "up to speed".' Listening is one of speed's victims.

> The reason why we have two ears, and only one mouth, is that we may listen the more, and talk the less.
>
> Zeno of Citium, to a youth who was talking nonsense. Quoted by Diogenes Laërtius, in the chapter on Zeno, in *Lives, Teachings, and Sayings of Famous Philosophers*

The healing quality of listening comes from giving a person time and attention: the listener's overall view of the speaker's life, and careful watching of the minutest detail – how the speaker is, from moment to moment. This fosters growth at both conscious and unconscious levels – deeper self-listening, increased self-esteem, and a surer sense of identity.

Ranking high among the personal gifts of the listener as healer is calmness. Calmness conveys balance and stability, gives some degree of peacefulness to those who are anxious, and yields poise: of manner, voice and body. The words 'poise', 'gravitas' and 'guru' stem, respectively, from 'weigh', 'weight' and 'weighty'. Thus different cultures, European and Eastern, speak of dignity in a similar way. And the mark of weighty dignity, one of its main attributes, and among the most healing of all qualities, is to be unhurried.

Listening aids self-awareness

Being listened to helps a person observe and regard himself anew. This observing may cast more light on costly habits and on negative patterns, inner and/or outer: patterns of thinking, feeling, and rigid moulds in the memory; patterns of attitude and mindset; patterns of reaction, behaviour and relating.

Hearing one's feelings and reflections spoken aloud – and accepted and reflected back by another person – enables worries, some of which may be deep seated and long held, to rise to the surface. This makes it easier to face and assess needs and problems, which can now be learned from and worked with. To hear one's own spoken thoughts, old and new, range across aspects of a problem, or a major life question, can bring clarity where once was confusion. From clarity comes conviction, choice, decision.

In this process of relooking and realigning, change may come, and perhaps some shedding and discarding of ways and habits no longer appropriate. Fresh insights may arise. But even if the speaker says nothing new, nothing they were not already aware of, this self-hearing may help them see themselves more accurately, more fully, so that they can confront life, and any future tests and challenges, with new vigour. The first step towards change is self-observation: honest, sometimes humbling, self-observation.

A listener of integrity will submit himself to the same inward looking. The distinguished, and justifiably feared, advocate, the late George Carman QC, when asked about his formula for success in court, replied, 'Hard work. Meticulous preparation and research. Dedication. Passionate commitment. A belief that a great responsibility rests upon your shoulders, in all your work on behalf of your clients. And a constant, vigilant self-criticism, to see and assess how you can improve.'

Obstacles to Good Listening

Listening is important to all of us, in various spheres of life: with members of our family, in social life, in a pastoral or, indeed, any professional role, and particularly in ministry and spiritual direction. The basics of good listening – found in the therapeutic model – can aid fuller listening in most forms of relationships: with friend, partner, parent, parishioner, teacher, work colleague. No matter how experienced we are, we can always learn to be better listeners.

It may be helpful for you to assess your own listening powers by considering the following typical obstacles, as prompts for self-enquiry, and to aid continuing self-observation while listening to people. For adults, relearning how to listen begins by unlearning: shedding negative habits and patterns, involving a fundamental re-examination of how we relate.

Body language

Be very watchful of your body language. Obstacles to good encounters include:

- A restless, fidgety manner

- Many glances at watch and/or clock

- Eye contact that is infrequent, or so long that it becomes a stare

- Breaking connection to check electronic devices, or worse, to take a call

Time pressure

If speaker and/or listener do not have enough time to meet at depth, and yet they meet anyway, one person (or both) is likely to feel impatient, thereby putting pressure on the speaker and hampering the encounter. To avoid disappointment or rush, both parties can be helped to articulate the amount of time they have available. Two of the preliminaries needed for real contact are a sense that the listener is trustworthy, and security of time.

Careful joint judgement is needed so that the length of each meeting does not overtax the concentration, emotional stamina and absorption rate of either person.

> May the God of steadfastness and encouragement
> grant you to live in harmony with one another ...
> Welcome one another, therefore, as Christ has
> welcomed you, for the glory of God.
>
> Romans 15:5,7

Distractions

These may come from external factors, such as the speaker's mannerisms, or from internal matters – the listener's thoughts and/or feelings, sometimes leading to self-preoccupation. These intrude on that inner space which is so necessary if one is to be receptive to another person.

Tiredness

The more tired you are, the more inappropriately verbal you may be, because so much energy and continuous self-observing is needed to attain, and then retain, an attentive stillness. This is especially hard when faced, for example, with a self-pitying tone or mood. Tiredness often leads to impatience, and to interventions that are too frequent and/or too long.

Tiredness also makes it much harder for a listener to bear a speaker's repetitions, such as when grieving, or after a shock or trauma, or if the speaker is stuck in a groove and seems unable to move on.

For these reasons, nothing is more important for relaxed, alert creative listening than the constant nurturing of one's own energy: physical, mental, emotional and spiritual. This requires space, inner and outer: time to rest and reflect; time to be renewed, in any wholesome way; time for the comfort of being listened to – by family and friends, by a work supervisor or counsellor, if necessary, and especially, if one has faith, by God.

Stock responses

'Don't worry,' is very often a verbal blemish, for two main reasons. Firstly, it may be heard by the speaker as presumptuous, patronising, possessive or invasive. Secondly, even when it is reasonable advice, it betokens a lack of empathy for, and understanding of, the speaker's own feelings of doubt or despair. We invest so much in our feelings. Even when seemingly wrong-headed or self-pitying, if feelings are not heeded and respected, then a large part of the speaker's identity is not being heard.

'I know how you must be feeling,' however well intentioned, is not a necessary statement. The speaker will know if you are with them, alongside them, at both emotional and intellectual levels. Verbal assertions and assurances of support count less than that more-profound reassurance received from your whole person and presence.

Superficial listening

One-dimensional listening attends only to the surface material, and to its overt message and more obvious signals. There could be many reasons for this, ranging from inexperience or relative lack of training as a listener, to a wish to avoid negative feelings and/or sad and painful subjects.

Diverting the speaker's line of thought

Some listeners have a tendency to intervene at a tangent, introducing a radically new topic (which the speaker is not at that moment ready to absorb and work with), rather than following one step behind the line and flow of the speaker's thoughts and feelings. In good listening, as in many areas of life, the timing is all.

Labelling

Labelling the speaker (either to oneself or verbally) as 'a worrier', or unduly 'anxious', is to be avoided. Preserving a flexible and adaptive view of the speaker allows room for potential and change. Watchfulness over what you say is important because, like material labels, verbal labels have strong adhesive and can get stuck in the speaker's mind, which may already feel bound and strapped by a negative self-image.

The listener's attitude is the primary factor: more crucial than choice of method or technique. The aim is to listen with the heart, and to listen to the heart.

Hippocrates famously said, 'I prefer to study the person who has a disease, rather than, primarily, the disease a person has.' A listener who values the person first, and sees the presenting problem as secondary and in relation to the person, gives the speaker space to relocate the central area of assessment and responsibility in the self, rather than in other people. The centre of gravity is moved from outside to inside.

The larger the emotional space, the more the speaker feels free to be himself. The ultimate aim of all rich relationships is to allow and encourage the other person to find and express their own voice, their God-given uniqueness. This is only possible in an atmosphere and climate of freedom, grace and spaciousness.

Judging

Moralising or being judgemental – outwardly or inwardly, or both – severely hampers the warm, open-hearted and tolerant attitude and acceptance which form the foundation of good listening, and of healthy encounters generally. Acceptance of the speaker includes their thoughts and feelings, their values, personality and behaviour. Even the internal type of moralising, which is not articulated, will be instinctively felt by the speaker, and will usually close off whole areas of self-disclosure. Where there is a spirit of mutual trust, the speaker may feel free to reveal personal material – such as sad memories, loss, guilt, shame or fears – possibly for the first time. This is one of the listener's prime privileges.

Compassion comes from escaping the narrowness of opposing categories: 'attractive' or 'unattractive', 'like' or 'dislike'. This relative detachment requires a balancing act, because it is part of our basic biological drive to be drawn towards beauty, truth and goodness. The listener needs to attend to their own emotions and reactions, but not be caught or trapped by them.

Any tendency towards moralising, or where the listener imposes their own values or standards, even in subtle ways, might prompt the listener to do more self-work: for example, seeing in the speaker unwanted aspects of themselves.

Projection

> Why do you see the speck in your brother's eye,
> but do not notice the log that is in your own eye?

Luke 6:41

Projection is, literally, throwing in front of oneself. It is the process by which specific wishes, impulses or other (usually unwanted) aspects of the self, inner and/or outer, are supposed or imagined, largely unconsciously, to be lodged exclusively in some other person or object.

Projection is preceded by what psychologists call 'denial' of the unwanted characteristic or impulse, and a desire to unburden and escape from one's shadow (or repressed) side. However, projection is sometimes a looking to another person or people, often in an idealised (and therefore unrealistic) way, to make up for longed-for qualities or positive attributes in oneself.

According to the ground-breaking theories and insights of the psychoanalyst Melanie Klein, the origin of projections can usually be traced to early babyhood, when the infant is being breastfed, and perceives the mother as having, and proffering, one good breast and one hateful or fearful breast.[6]

Transference

Transference can be described as a wholesale form of projection. It is the re-enactment, generally as repair work, of a previous relationship, usually with a parent or a sibling. In transference, the speaker displaces on to the listener aspects of,

---

[6] Melanie Klein, 'Our Adult World and Its Roots in Infancy' in *Envy and Gratitude and Other Works 1946–1963* (London: Vintage Press, 1997), pp. 247-264.

and feelings about, a person who was, or still is, important and significant.

The essence of transference is that the speaker views and treats the listener, especially in the early stages of their relationship, as if they were the person towards whom the original, intense emotions were felt. This person, who is being displaced or transferred, can be a positive or a negative figure: friendly and benign or cursed and resented. Transference is an unconscious ploy to draw (or drag) another person into the drama of one's life.

The listener will experience their own counter-transference (the reactions and fantasies evoked by encountering the other), and will do well to listen to and register these – both as prompts to self-work and as the most valuable sources of information about the speaker's current difficulties and manner of relating to significant others.

Typecasting

Typecasting people and/or situations leads to assumptions which may not be on target, and to a tendency to think in terms of stereotypes, thus missing the speaker's individuality and uniqueness, or the complexity of the scenario under consideration.

> What thing so good which not some disharmony bring?

> William Alexander, *Darius*, 'Chorus'

Just as failure brings challenges, so does success. There is no unmixed blessing. A new opportunity may be seen by the speaker in an ambivalent way: as a potential test or threat, as well as possible joy. No gain is risk free. And so, for example, when hearing about an engagement or a pregnancy, a listener would do well to blend congratulations with careful, waiting observation for any underlying apprehensions.

Statements

When listening to adults, open questions should usually be chosen, in preference to making statements and assumptions. For example, to say to someone as a greeting, 'You are looking well,' is well meant, but could be premature. The person's appearance may be better than their health, feelings or circumstances.

If the listener makes a statement, this carries a risk. It may rob the speaker of self-discovering by describing things in his own way and in his own words. Continuous self-discovery (by both participants) is the most rich and rewarding element in the whole process of dialogue.

There is another reason why questions should precede statements. You may not be an accurate reader of another person's feelings. Appearance may be worse than reality. For example, what may seem to you like a depressed tone of voice may just be a sign of tiredness. To label feelings inaccurately is to cast oneself as 'the authority' on another's inner world. To do so may recapitulate a misnaming of feelings by parent figures, leading a person to doubt and distrust his own reading of his emotional life.

Questions posed with a sense of genuine interest and in an open-ended way, such as, 'How are you?' or 'How are you feeling?' are to be preferred to 'You sound …' or, 'Are you …?' Let the speaker identify and describe their own feelings, in their own way and time.

If and when the listener comments, they should gently nudge. Where possible, a would-be statement should be rephrased into the form of question. An unselfish listener has an aim, and one aim only: assisting the speaker to interpret self to self.

Being listened to with deep attention is a life-changing and a life-enhancing adventure; an inner journey of joy and self-discovery; a finding of one's authentic, original self, freed at last of conditioning – by family, schooling, workplace, society's trends and fashions and shallow values. This is the route to true liberation.

> In the cloud of the human soul,
> there is a fire stronger than the lightning,
> and a grace more precious than the rain.

> Ruskin, 'The Mystery of Life and its Art', *Sesame and Lilies*

Proving oneself

Probably the biggest and most frequent trap for a listener is over-activity. This is often triggered when a speaker seems stuck in a life groove. The listener may mistakenly see this impasse as a reflection of his own ineffectiveness in the relationship, and – to prove themselves – an insecure listener may try to force change, or the pace of change.

What my analyst once said about psychotherapy applies, with equal wisdom, to listening in any form or setting: 'You achieve more by doing less.' When my wife asked my analyst shortly before she died what was the essence of good psychotherapy, she replied, 'The listening and the observing are the most important part.'

Total listening or complete cure are not realistic goals. Often, the most you can jointly achieve is for the speaker to face, accept and come to terms with past and/or present grief or pain or illness. Whatever resists cure will have to be more patiently endured – perhaps for the rest of one's life.

Always remember and keep in mind that you are not the prime healing factor. Inwardly kneeling at the feet of your Maker, and being open to His power and mercy, you are a channel of God-given insight and compassion flowing through you.

Advice

A core danger of advice is that it may be based on what has worked for the listener or for someone known to them. These solutions and ways forward may not be appropriate for the speaker. Another major disadvantage of advice is that it tends to foster dependence.

Rather than give advice, especially if unsought by the speaker, the furthest a listener should usually go is to review options with the speaker, so that the speaker can decide and determine their own path, however slowly and unsteadily, and however painful the journey. In the charting of their own path, they may become a more able and more aware advice-giver to themselves. The long-term goal is to strengthen the speaker's confidence in making choices and decisions.

Responses which encourage self-listening, self-awareness and self-expression are more enabling than directional guidance. Such responses by the listener assist newness, self-finding, adventure into the self, more sense of self-worth, and tolerance of one's limitations.

A listener who is non-possessive and non-authoritarian is content to be a catalyst, respecting the autonomy of the speaker as a self-directing person. The core and essence of good listening is to support and accompany the speaker while they connect or reconnect with their own unique wisdom and self-belief. What Schnabel says of teaching music is true for anyone in a helping role: 'What can a teacher do? At the best open a door; but the student has to pass through it.'

The adventure of self-discovery has much in common with creative processes: these recapitulate the spontaneity and the spirit of exploration found in childhood learning, with its increasing sense of power and mastery.

Controlling

There are many drawbacks if a listener tries to direct the course and shape of an encounter. To be asked leading (rather than follow-up) questions may be felt by the speaker as intrusive, even invasive, putting them on the defensive, and hindering free and open self-expression and self-disclosure. The topic which the listener thinks is interesting or important may not be the subject of paramount concern to the speaker.

Creative listening does not use or abuse power, or even seek power. Listening, when dedicated to its true purpose and vocation, uses its innate strength to empower.

> The greatest good you can do for another is not just share your riches, but to reveal to him his own.

> Benjamin Disraeli

Doing

If you are too much in the mode of doing/advising, you may be avoiding your own feelings and memories. In effect, you are saying to yourself, 'I won't let your hurt remind me of my hurt.' An over-emphasised helper role creates a duality, a gap, between the supposedly strong helper and the supposedly weaker recipient. This gap reinforces dependence. Dependence hampers growth in each of the two people, as individuals, and distorts the balance of their working relationship.

A good listener is reliable and dependable, ready to yield the ego's desire to control, and thus willing to let go graciously when the span of meetings comes to a natural end. The central aim of an unselfish listener is to reinforce the speaker's own authority and originality, and to elicit the speaker's innate wisdom so that the speaker may listen to their inner voice, and their own wisdom, and learn from it.

Keep replacing the anxiety, or compulsion, to *do* with the courage to *be*.

Seeking solutions

The listener may see a valid solution to a problem, sometimes weeks or months before the speaker. This possible solution is often best kept unspoken, so that the speaker does their own finding, in their own way and at their own pace. Strong growth needs, depends on, strong roots.

Self-realised solutions are more readily owned and acted upon, and are more likely to bring long-term benefits than the adoption of what someone else suggests – however respected and experienced the other person is, however useful the suggestions, and even though there might be short-term gains for the speaker if the listener were to offer advice.

The listener will therefore be reluctant to relate how they or someone they know has coped or dealt with a similar situation. What worked for one person may not work for another; and being offered a ready-made, second-hand idea may, then or later, be likely to erode the speaker's sense of their own uniqueness.

Education and business life foster, encourage and reward problem-solving: the search for practical and pragmatic answers. But some parts of an individual person's life pattern resist outer change, and thus resist solutions. In some cases, the most to be aimed for is a shift in attitude towards more understanding and acceptance, coming to terms both with one's own limitations and with the constraint of circumstances.

Salvation does not necessarily or always come in the form of solution. But it may be healing if the speaker shares with the listener their own sense of the scale and intensity of a life problem, and its seemingly impenetrable or intractable nature. Hope comes not only from finding meaning, but also from bonding and belonging, having a fellow traveller by one's side, and feeling understood, respected and accepted.

Expectations

Lightly held hopes by the listener are a vital part of the tone and quality of relaxed concentration and hovering attention. It is one thing to have lightly held hopes for the well-being of another person's life. It is quite another thing for a listener to bring to a relationship their own expectations, such as about the possibility of change or the pace of change.

The safest and soundest approach is consistently to leave to the speaker the core initiatives, such as aspects of decision-making and the choice of main subjects or themes within each encounter and in the overall relationship. *The listener's central focus should be on care, not cure.*

Expectation often has two main defects: being too rigid and too high. By contrast, hopes tend to have a living, flickering quality, but may nonetheless be deeply ingrained and influential in the psyche (in a positive, life-giving way). Hopes nourish if they retain some flexibility – lightly clasped, not tightly gripped. Expectation narrows; hope widens.

Over-reacting

Just as an instrumental player creates a musical note from a wide spectrum of sound, from very soft to very loud, so also does a person-to-person listener have all-important choices to make: not only whether and when to speak, but also, for each response or intervention, to grade and select with care the strength or weight of expression – as to tone and content. The potential range extends from the subtle and allusive to the overt and blatant.

A frequent error of technique is to make an over-stated response. Over-reacting – especially if the topic is emotive – may result in the listener taking a position or stance that is difficult to amend or retreat from. By contrast, an under-stated response, at least initially, is almost always safe: it enables the listener to find the appropriate tone during future exchanges, and it gives emotional space to the speaker.

Research shows how quickly reactive are body and mind to threat, actual or possible. Studies of psychogalvanic skin response[7] have shown how sensitively people respond to even a minor lessening of the listener's degree of acceptance, or to a single word which, in meaning and/or in the tone spoken, is only slightly stronger than the feelings the speaker is currently experiencing.

Over-identifying

A listener should avoid extremes: being too distant from or too close to the speaker, or to the mood or content of the encounter. A frequent danger for a listener is in being over-stimulated by what is said. This over-involvement may come, for example, from curiosity about some aspects of the material; or because something said jars or offends; or, which often happens, what is being shared makes an echo in the listener's memories.

If you do hear such an echo from your own life, past and/or present, you can usefully draw from your own experiences: the use of memory can assist you in showing empathy. But at the same time, keep in your mind and approach a clear distinction between yourself and the other person, between your life and the equally unique life of the speaker. And be especially careful, when you find parallels, to avoid the trap of projecting causes and outcome from your own experiences on to the other person.

Over-tiredness is often a sign, a warning, of being emotionally over-involved, or of being too active during meetings, or both.

---

[7] This measures changes in the electrical properties of the skin in response to changes to stimulus.

Let each of you look not only to his own interests,
but also to the interests of others.

Philippians 2:4

Unintegrated parts of self

Aspects of oneself can get in the way of pure listening and of
true, unimpeded encounter. Such obstacles might include an
unfulfilled side of yourself which you are attempting to live
out, vicariously, in and through the speaker; or an insecure side
which seeks false power by wanting to control, or even
dominate; or a defended side, an unwanted part of yourself; or
a sore spot, which shies away from discussion, or perhaps the
very mention, of some particular subjects.

Listening is challenging and potentially life-enhancing, not
only for the speaker but also for the listener. Listening inspires
work that is never ending: constant self-listening, willing and
brave self-learning, resulting in continuous self-healing. The
speaker will sense, and may grow stronger from knowing, that
the learning in and from these encounters can be a two-way
process.

The healing elements of listening include not only what
happens in the speaker – catharsis, the unblocking and easing
of repressed memories, insight, integration, more sense of
identity and self-esteem – but also the degree of relatedness the
two people attain, often while or after walking together along
awkward paths, sometimes bumpy, sometimes steep.

And the healing includes the amount and degree of self-
work which each person stimulates in the other. Extending
Jung's famous dictum, 'Only the wounded healer heals,' it is
true to say that only the continuously being-healed person
heals.

Silence

*Now when Job's three friends heard of all this evil
that had come upon him, they ... made an
appointment together to come to condole with him
and comfort him. ... And they sat with him on the
ground seven days and seven nights, and no one
spoke a word to him, for they saw that his suffering
was very great.*

Job 2:11-13

We only begin to have a real and deep relationship with
someone when we understand their silences. Understanding
silences means respecting them, learning to read them, and
reacting to them in an apt way.

In any form of pastoral work, this means allowing the
speaker to break most of the silences. This ensures that the
speaker retains control over the encounter's flow, content and
direction. To honour this approach demands deep reserves of
patience in a listener. For example, people who are depressed
will often take time both to formulate thoughts and to express
them.

Some listeners fear silence. They think their role during
silence is inactive, perhaps even ineffective. This is probably
the very opposite of the reality: the profound worth of sharing
someone's silence. Therefore St James counsels, 'Let every man
be quick to hear, slow to speak' (James 1:19).

Silences are also testing for the speaker. Silences compel a
likely confrontation with the unexpected, and also the as yet
half-realised. Being with someone in outer quietness means

waiting for memories, words, feelings, insight and sometimes tears to emerge.

This patient 'being-with' silence also means trusting in the power and value of silence: a time for sifting, sorting, healing and the freedom simply to be – a precious, even if temporary, release from the noise, stress and frenetic pace of so much of everyday life.

Listening to words is a form of doing, and a most demanding form – as is listening to silence. Being-with *is* active. And this sense of a deeply shared experience will be felt and appreciated by both speaker and listener. Seen truly, silence is opportunity, not obstacle. The deeper the silence, the richer will be the words that are conceived and born from that silence. And the deeper the silence, the more apt and astute is one's sense of timing.

> Who can wait the moment of maturity – in speaking, writing, acting and giving – will have nothing to retract, and little to repent of.

Lavater[8]

Longer silences tend to have special significance. If the listener attends to them, and enters them fully, they will not feel compelled to fill longer silences with words. Instead, they will regard the silence as in itself full. To refrain from outward action is sometimes the hardest, but also potentially the most fruitful, of all aspects of a relationship.

Involved detachment

> I have seen many who were saved by silence, but none who were saved by chatter.

St Ambrose

---

[8] Johann Lavater, *Aphorisms on Man* (London: J. Johnson, 1791).

By taking a stance of relative silence, the listener attends with more clarity – to the speaker and to himself. And they will listen with more patience and more tolerance.

By examining the urge to speak – seeking to read the motive beneath the yet-to-be-expressed word content – the listener can detect and hush elements of ego and vanity, speed or slickness, opinions and preoccupations, prejudice and censoriousness, and any desire to influence or even dominate. Then the listener's words will arise out of inner silence, not from emotional confusion or a mental whirlpool. The listener can thus observe and cherish the other person, in all the depth and richness of their individual nature. And, most crucially, the listener will have set an atmosphere of space, freedom and warm openness.

One of the favourite dicta of St Ambrose, Bible scholar and Bishop of Milan, was by a fellow saint, Seraphim of Sarov. St Seraphim was a remarkable man: monk, mystic, spiritual director and a confessor respected for his insight into the conscience of penitents. Before embarking on pastoral ministry, Seraphim spent 25 years as a hermit, living in a forest hut. He was dedicated and single-minded in everything he did. One of his ascetic disciplines (in common with some other saints of the Orthodox tradition) was to kneel on a stone for many days in a row, absorbed in prayer. The saying of his which Ambrose so admired was, 'Silence is the cross on which man must crucify his ego.'

The exercise (or feat) of involved detachment helps the listener to respond rather than react. Why is it important to distinguish between reaction and response? Reaction tends to be jumpy; response is poised and considered, and is preceded (often, but not necessarily always) by pause and reflection. Reaction can therefore be superficial; response, by contrast, arises from the depths of the self. Reaction reflects and represents only a small part of a person, whereas response comes from the whole being. Last, and vitally, response is the more other-focused.

Here, then, is the basic rule for a listener: silence, until a temporarily better good is served by speech.

> I have often regretted my speech, but never my silence.
>
> Publilius Syrus, *The Moral Sayings of Publilius Syrus: a Roman Slave*, Maxim 1,070

Aspects of Good Listening and Responding

The following observations are relevant for many types of meeting: formal or informal, regular or infrequent.

Setting

The quality of encounter depends not only on interaction, verbal and non-verbal, but also on care in preparing the setting. For formal pastoral encounters, consider:

- Surroundings that convey an atmosphere of calm and privacy

- Lighting

- Temperature

- A warmly decorated room

- No intervening desk or table

- Comfortable seating, of similar height, with appropriate distance between speaker and listener: far enough to safeguard emotional space; close enough for good contact

- Forethought about possible interruptions or phone calls. Nothing is more destructive to deep speaking and listening than a noisy setting, or a meeting place vulnerable to interruptions.

Dependence

Especially in the early weeks of a series of meetings, the person seeking help is likely to try to project authority and a role as problem-solver on to the listener. A non-possessive, empowering listener will resist these projections. The listener may enquire whether there is an element of transference (recapitulating patterns from another relationship) on the part of the speaker in these projections.

In therapy, a frequent early-stage problem and challenge is to coax forth any ambivalence and all mixed feelings in the speaker. If not soon brought to the surface, these thoughts will fester and grow, and may even become explosive, resulting in a powerful negative transference.

In addition, the listener will redirect attempts to project and devolve authority on to the shoulders of the speaker, thereby helping the speaker to tap into strength and authority internally. The word 'authority' comes from the Latin verb for 'to increase'. The speaker is thereby empowered to unearth his own originality, his unique character and qualities, and to set free his strength and find his distinct direction and destiny in life.

Dependence delays or defeats the central role of listening, which is *to enable*. The role and aim of creative listening is to empower the speaker to unfold, to believe in and to make full use of his own wisdom.

It is the greatest possible privilege to be invited to be a companion on another person's (often complex) journey of self-exploration. A creative listener will help the speaker see himself not as static, not as permanently shaped and moulded by his past, but as a living, evolving personality.

Active listening fosters the joint work and discovery (often unexpected) of deep, long-buried memories and material, and attends to nuances in the subtle shifts of words, body language and emotional tone.

View the listening relationship within the whole context and time frame of the speaker's life, and ask yourself, 'Why are they coming here and opening up, now? Will they eventually have more to bring than the presenting problem?'

Also see the relationship as potentially a part of your own life and development by considering, 'Why is this person coming to talk with me? What can they, and this particular meeting, teach me about life and about myself?' An open and humble attitude such as this bridges any power gap there may be in the mind of the speaker or the listener, or both, and lessens any distinction between helper and helped.

Uniqueness

Preserve a sense of this person's uniqueness. Come afresh to each person, each encounter. In short, make every moment count. Respecting the uniqueness of the other person means trying to see things from the speaker's viewpoint, and asking yourself, 'How is this particular person feeling and responding to this particular memory or event or problem?'

The main way to respect uniqueness is to work with whatever the speaker brings, allowing them to choose the content, and by seeking with them to understand the reasons for the emotional tone.

Respect the speaker's current level and degree of insight. Go with the pace of growth they are ready for. Wait for the germination. The speaker's psyche contains the seeds of change. The role of the listener is to assist the speaker by attending with them to the inner stirrings of their own potential, as they befriend themselves.

Good listening is open and receptive: coming to each moment of each encounter without preconceptions, without imposing or forcing, being ready for the unexpected. The creative tone of such listening has an unmistakable feel, for the listener and the speaker, endowing their encounter with an adventurous, explorative edge.

Focus

Attend to whatever content the speaker brings: simple and homely topics as well as the dramatic and the potentially life-changing. This entails listening to the speaker in all their diversity: hope and fear, heart and reason, vulnerable or buoyant, the inner child and the adult self.

The listener needs to keep in close touch with their own values and beliefs, their standards of conduct, and the scale of importance they place on issues, so as not to blur the distinction between self and other as the relationship grows and evolves. At the same time, the listener will respect the speaker's authority and autonomy, and the degree of importance the speaker attaches to whatever they talk about, and to the feelings they bring and share: problems, doubts, worries, joys and memories with a wide range of different colourings.

Content has layers. Avoid the temptation to attend only to the overt and initial presenting problem(s), and/or to the speaker's questions about their own life, or life in general.

In order not to miss vital issues and deeper layers of material yet to surface, the listener needs to listen to their own instinct, intuition and messages from the unconscious, as well as to communications from the speaker's unconscious.

Multidimensional listening

Philip Larkin wrote about his friend, the novelist Barbara Pym, and the quality of their dialogue (the *Dictionary of National Biography: 1971–1980*). He chose for special praise not sharpness of wit, not her command of the English language, not her descriptive and narrative powers. Instead, he remarked on 'the gentle watchfulness of her conversation'.

Observe not only what is said but also how it is said. And pay as much, if not more, attention to feelings as to facts. Clarify and help to draw out ambivalence and mixed feelings. And be in no hurry to help resolve this conflict in the speaker, even if it causes much tension between the two of you. The reason and purpose for such a painful and testing, yet finally creative, delay of reconciliation is to allow enough material and examples to emerge, so that the speaker, in their own time and at their pace, comes to see and realise their origin in the speaker's own unconscious. By gradually learning to accept and own both negative and positive feelings, the speaker then has the best chance and opportunity to use and integrate their limitations and strength.

Good listening, in addition to being open, is wide and deep: wide in scope; deep in the number of levels being 'gently watched'. Listen not only with the outer ear, and not only with your mind and your understanding, but also, and especially, with your inner ear, your whole person, attending to another whole person – mind to mind, heart to heart, soul to soul. Humility leads to a right degree of closeness and intimacy.

Remembering the chastening lesson in the story in the introduction to this book of Martin Buber and his visitor, listen not only to the presenting problem(s), nor just to surface content, but also to underlying doubts and concerns, and to life questions as yet unformulated and/or unspoken: questions a person has not consciously asked himself, let alone posed and shared with anyone else. It was said of Socrates that he helped his interlocutors each to give birth to their own thought.

Attend not only to what is being said, but also – and especially – to what is not said. Deep listening reads between the lines. This involves observing – with the whole of yourself – the following:

- The spoken words

- The way speech is delivered, noting changes in voice, such as speed, tone or volume

- Hesitations, sighs, shudders

- Unfinished sentences or thoughts

- What precedes and what follows silence

- The mood, the feeling-tone, of silences

- Words, feelings, subjects or ideas, events or experiences which are repeated or emphasised or given greater air time

- Stories told/reports about others, or picked up on from the news, which may serve as a projective screen for the speaker's own feelings

- Forgetting: events or periods that cannot be clearly remembered

- Gestures as well as the most subtle messages of body language: these movements are the deepest, the most unconscious, and thus the most revealing

- Any discord between what is being said and the accompanying body language

- Freudian slips

- The unspoken question or memory

- Unconscious processes

Observe the content of what is shared, the timing (within the encounter, and in the context of the relationship), and seek the meaning.

In addition to all these items for observation (of the speaker and the dialogue), it is vital for the listener to constantly monitor and adjust their own reactions, inner and outer. Thus the careful and caring watching of the speaker is put into a wider frame, a quasi-simultaneous triple watch:

- What is going on in the speaker?

- What is going on in me, the listener?

- What is going on between us, in the relationship?

Each of these three areas for observation has an inner and an outer dimension. This triple (or, rather, sixfold) watching helps to keep the listener on a middle path, between the extremes of aloofness and over-involvement. And the middle path gives the listener a right-distanced stance in relating to the speaker, the content, the listener's own reactions and the overall relationship.

Multidimensional listening needs fully as much concentration as a surgeon uses when performing an operation.

Naturalness of pace

To the blind man near Jericho, Christ asked, 'What do you want me to do for you?' (Luke 18:41). With His divine insight, Christ knew the man's need, his hope and his wish. But with sensitivity and with gentleness of pace, He encouraged the man to articulate his need for healing.

A skilled listener may sense – sometimes months before the speaker – the cause of a problem, as well as the possible outcome and ways forward, but will allow the speaker to come to their own understanding and to find their own direction – in their own way and at their own pace.

When attained, intimacy energises. But the joint path towards intimacy needs to be walked with delicacy, balancing openness with gradualness of pace, and matching boldness and risk with care and caution.

The broad pattern of maturing of character – based on real, solid, lasting growth – evolves gradually. Much of what people need and seek, they already have in them. It is what, deep down, they know and are.

Self-discovery, even if delayed, is usually worth more, and is more readily owned and accepted and acted upon, than receiving another person's view, advice or guidance, however valid and accurate the view, however useful the advice, and no matter how much the listener is trusted. Not only is self-discovery more readily accepted and used, but the fruits of self-discovery also endure.

Line

A person who has natural gifts as a listener will have, and seek to preserve, what musicians call 'a good sense of line'. Composers give line to their music by balancing sound and silence, notes and rests, combined with rhythmic impetus and harmonic progression. These bring flow to the music, a reaching forward, an 'onwardness'. And the wide-hearing performer or conductor will, from the very beginning of a work, have a sense of the end, the culmination.

In performance, good line begins with care for the texture and proportion of phrases. Musicians usually take a long, deep breath as guide for the length of phrases, because, of all instruments, the human voice is the nearest to nature.

A musician with a sense of good line then relates phrases to themes/subjects, subjects to sections, sections to the movement, and the movements to the work as a whole. This linking results in a natural unfolding of the music, an unfolding with three main qualities: freshness and a spirit of recreation combined with a feeling of musical inevitability.

The aim of good line is to produce a seamless experience. To use another image, good line delights in detail of contour, and also reveals, from the very first bar, the stature and cohesion of the architecture of the music, as a complete and unified work.

How can line in music serve as a model for line in person-to-person listening? Sensitivity-to-line in listening involves staying close to the emerging flow of material from the speaker – the content, both the overt and the subtle (or subtext); never forcing or imposing; drawing from a deep well of patience; and with a constant quelling of those of your thoughts which are formulating replies or questions, until both instinct and intellect confirm to you that it would be wise and helpful to speak: wise, on grounds of timing; helpful, because of the possible value to the dialogue of what you are to say or ask.

Horizontal or vertical listening?

One other aspect of listening aids good line: sensing when to listen vertically and when to listen horizontally. The horizontal is outer, linear and chronological. The vertical ranges more widely, as well as more rapidly, between past, present and future.

The difference can be illustrated by an exchange I had with a client some years ago. He spoke of his anger at not being able to send an urgent letter by Royal Mail because of a strike by postal workers. His father and brother were postmen, and so this was a very real family and financial difficulty, as well as a personal, practical problem.

I was alert to the possible need for vertical listening, should he wish to talk about the strike and its impact on his family. My silence allowed him to continue, and he soon made clear that his intention at this session was to mention the strike only in passing, as one of several examples of being baulked and frustrated by events: he spoke of a feeling of trying to swim against a strong tide. Everything seemed to be going wrong for him. This was a signal for me to listen horizontally – primarily. Primarily, because wide-span listening is to some extent tuned simultaneously to both the vertical and the horizontal. It was not until a later session that we were to make direct use of the postbox metaphor, as a symbol of his sexual difficulties in his marriage.

I try now to be more aware of how a client might use a follow-up question. This form of intervention can either stimulate 'vertical', analytic thinking, or it can foster the flow of a 'horizontal' (more intuitive and associative) process.

Hearing and listening

Hearing and listening, different but related, have kinship with the difference between surface and depth. The aim is to hear facts and listen for feelings; to hear detail and listen for pattern.

You hear, but do you also listen? And do you listen to what you hear?

You hear the sound of a voice, but are you also listening to what musicians call, such as in a quartet, the 'inner voices'?

Hearing employs the outer ear. Listening uses the inner ear and involves the whole person: the formal training you may have had in listening skills; all of the informal, yet vital, teaching of your life experience; and all the attentiveness you are giving to this person at this moment.

Understanding

An able listener understands. They, as it were, 'stand under'. For the speaker, feelings that are understood offer space, freedom and opportunity: to find potential amid doubt and danger, and when faced with differences and difficulty; space in which to make choices and to take alternative courses of action and behaviour; an insightful distance, so as to withdraw projections from other people; courage to delve below the surface and to ask basic questions about one's own life, and about life itself.

And being understood invites a loosening, a lessening of limitations, as well as growth and development of qualities, talents and abilities. Being understood calms uncertainty and turmoil, restores inner and outer harmony, revitalises strength and energy, and emboldens one to grow in and through all of life's experiences.

To be heard, with alertness and at depth, by the listener's inner ear, assists the speaker in his search for meaning, purpose and direction. The speaker seeks, as we all do, enlightenment. Where am I? Who am I? Who and what do I live for? On what ground do I stand? On which paths shall I walk?

Hearing the main themes

Luke 18:18-23 tells of Christ's meeting with a rich young man. They speak together about the commandments, but Christ, listening between the lines, then speaks of this man's central problem: his love of wealth.

With experience, you learn how to avoid being submerged by detail, and how to gauge the speaker's main need(s), which may vary from one encounter to another. Main needs include, for example, unburdening or catharsis, support and affirmation, and clarification.

Experience also helps the listener to avoid premature focus on particular issues, some of which may turn out to be of only passing interest and importance. Premature focus often leads to premature responses or interventions.

To prevent this, try to stay relatively quiet during the first half of the meeting, by which time you may hear main themes emerging. Some of your possible comments, questions or reflections may be kept in mind for use, if apt, at a future meeting. Indeed, by the end of a meeting, some of them may already have been dealt with, without any prompting by you.

And be alert for new – and perhaps crucial – issues to be raised just before the end – even as the person gets up to leave, or is at the door. These topics may form part of the agenda at a subsequent meeting if you are given a cue – depending, as always, on the speaker's own choice of the main ground for the two of you to traverse together.

Dialogue is existential: the answer to the question, 'What are the main themes in my life at present?' may emerge and be articulated by the speaker only during an encounter, or after later reflection and outside of your meetings together.

Stance

Watch and respect the pace of each encounter. And observe its shape; or, if the speaker's material is fragmentary, its relative lack of shape.

Good listening avoids the extremes of possessiveness and passivity. Both hinder the speaker's growth in confidence and in attaining a secure identity. Therefore, watch all the time the emotional distance between the two of you. Here, balance is symbolised by the listener's eye contact – steady but not staring, attentive but not intrusive.

Prayer can help give a listener the inner space for pausing before speaking, so that a detached involvement can be maintained. Constant self-monitoring is the mark and essence of a good listener. Yet self-monitoring can inhibit good listening, if the watchfulness is either too self-critical, self-preoccupied or too active, during an encounter.

A good listener is authentic, available and alongside:

> Participation in the joys and griefs of others is proof of your humanity and your religion.

> Lavater[9]

The speaker will be influenced not only by what he hears, but as much, and often more, by the listener's non-verbal

---

[9] *Aphorisms on Man.*

signals and communications: the way of sitting, gestures, eye contact, and facial expressions, such as a glance of understanding or a look of compassion.

Above all, the speaker will be influenced by the listener's whole attitude and bearing: their strong and humble self-assurance, quality of attention, stillness (inner and outer), reliability and consistency, and trustworthiness. And the speaker will be helped by someone with a warm and accepting approach, someone who believes in them.

Responses

> For everything there is a season ... a time to keep silence, and a time to speak.
>
> Ecclesiastes 3:1,7

Wait for a natural pause, so that you do not interrupt. So far as is possible, your responses or questions should be brief, lucid and phrased in an open-ended way (see next section), so that the speaker can project on to your response or question their own thoughts, feelings and sense of direction.

Often use and reflect back the speaker's own words and phrases, from the current meeting or from previous ones. This verbal mirroring (so long as it is not parroting back) brings various benefits. It confirms to the speaker that what they say is being heard accurately, and is also remembered and respected.

When you cross-refer to the speaker's earlier comments and statements, you show the quality of both your attentiveness and your memory, and this facilitates bonding and relating. It also reinforces the speaker's sense of self and self-worth.

It will also help the speaker if, from time to time, you paraphrase what they have said: this may give them a new angle for reflection. With experience, you will learn to tailor your language to suit the understanding and comprehension of each individual you meet.

Some of the listener's most helpful insights and contributions may be those which arise spontaneously, those which are unexpected and unplanned. The better the rapport, and the deeper the speaker's needs, the more likely this is to happen.

A good relationship facilitates, and makes more frequent, the speaker's tapping into unconscious material. Rapport also brings occasions when speaker and listener both think about the same thing at about the same time.

Thoughts and wording which occur spontaneously to the listener will still need to be briefly monitored before being expressed. Coming as a surprise to both the listener and speaker, they add freshness and new insight to the dialogue.

Take due care, but do not worry or be over-concerned about the how or what or when of your speaking. Listen inwardly for the voice of the Spirit of God, which will be speaking in you, to you and for you, when and while you are in the very midst of dialogue (Matthew 10:19-20).

Open questions

Some doctors begin a consultation by asking, 'How can I help?' This puts the accent and emphasis on the helper, rather than them staying in an empowering role. Keep in mind the distinction between a leading question and a follow-up question. Leading questions often breach the usual safe guideline of allowing the speaker to set the agenda.

I recall a very fine country doctor of the old school. He had a lively interest in psychology, made frequent home visits, and was attuned to the ways in which family dynamics and interaction impact on bodily and emotional health. His standard opener was, 'How is life treating you?' This question places responsibility outside of the self. Neither this question nor 'How can I help?' is open ended.

An alternative way of starting would be for the doctor not to pose an opening question, nor even to be the first to begin speaking. The creative alternative would be quiet, alert waiting.

Once dialogue has begun, apt questions can help the speaker gain new insight. Questions posed by a good listener will be open ended – open in two ways: not angling for a particular answer, and calling for more than a 'yes' or 'no' reply.

In social conversation, for example, an opening question, such as, 'How's work?' or, 'Are you busy?' put to someone currently preoccupied with family or health, finances or a forthcoming holiday, has the effect of directing the agenda. By contrast, 'How are you?' posed with sincere purpose and a listening ear, would be open ended.

With questions, there are degrees of open or closed, dependent on wording, timing and tone.

Start and end

A therapy session benefits from a framework of silence, starting and ending with the listener's silence. At the beginning of each meeting, a listening silence gives the speaker space, freedom and choice: three qualities of atmosphere which will pervade and govern the whole encounter.

The listener's silence at the end allows the speaker to stay with, to experience and to begin working on thoughts and feelings, some of them perhaps new. Conversely, a listener's parting words – especially certain forms of reassurance, such as advice not to worry – may be perceived by the speaker as somewhat superficial, and they may represent an attempted verbal flight from the listener's tension or anxiety about what they have heard. This tension may stem from linking what they have heard to something in their own life, and/or from uncertainty about whether the meetings can assist the magnitude of the speaker's needs. A safer mode for the listener at the time of parting is the silence of quiet, respectful solidarity. By honouring the other person, you may help them to honour themselves.

Self-integration

Early in my working life, I was a work-study engineer; before that, a music critic. Here are some of the aspects of listening which reflect those two sides of my background and personality, two sides which some readers may identify in themselves:

Engineer	Music critic
outer life	inner life
active	receptive (which is active, in its own way)
vocal/verbal	quiet
intellectual/analytic	intuitive/reflective
converger (in thought-patterns)	diverger
practical in orientation	attentive to feelings, relationships, communication
makes plans	goes with the flow
seeks solutions	wishes to assist others in finding their own answers

Good listening needs and uses – and will help develop – all of your skills and all of your talents, provided that their various facets are kept in balance. The best way to achieve and preserve balance is to keep watch on how long you stay in any one mode of your personality.

Care over essentials

Significantly, the first word of St Benedict's Rule is, 'Listen'. Good listening does not come from doing special things, but rather from doing a number of things with extraordinary care:

- Being reliable, such as keeping appointments and being on time

- Respecting confidentiality

- Not breaching defences, such as by over-reacting, over-interpreting, intrusive questioning, or by excess of words and ideas

- Tolerating, not judging, feelings, values or behaviour

- Seeing and understanding the speaker in the way they are seeing and experiencing self

- Showing empathy

- Being calm and emotionally steady

- Clarifying or summarising, when appropriate

- Being sensitive to memories, thoughts, feelings, fears and hopes that are just below the surface

- Encouraging an increase in the speaker's self-awareness; being with them at the growing edge of their psyche

- Being self-accepting, open and undefended. This will help elicit similar tendencies in the speaker, both in meetings with the listener and in other relationships

- Genuineness

Ask yourself why you are encountering this person now. And also be open to what you may be able to learn – from them and from the relationship – about self and about others.

Listening to yourself

Skills and techniques can be learned, and can help to improve the quality and depth of listening. But, ultimately, being a good listener is like being a good artist: what you do stems from who you are and how you are.

Your listening comes from your totality: your integrity, how you treat others, your self-knowledge, how you live your life, how you regard and treat yourself. When you have found in yourself the whole, the original, the genuine and authentic, you are readier to see and affirm these qualities in other people.

A healthy degree of self-liking aids and underpins the acceptance and loving of others. Self-liking comes in part from self-listening and self-learning, which in turn increase our insight into others and our capacity to learn from them.

Self-listening builds intuition – another essential aid in pastoral encounters (indeed, in any encounter). People seem to vary in their capacity for intuition, but it can be developed. Prerequisites for intuition are inner quiet and inner space.

Contact with nature can relieve stress and tension, and bring the ease and alert relaxation that lie at the heart of good listening. And prayer opens the deepest layers of the psyche – to the sphere and dimensions of the collective and the Transcendent. Listening to God (if you have faith) precedes and nurtures the quality of your listening to other people.

Deep listening involves the whole person: spiritual, intuitive, emotional, instinctive, intellectual, aesthetic. And so all forms of self-development, renewal and self-nourishing will enrich your listening: friendships, religion, psychotherapy, love of nature, the arts, hobbies, sport.

Every aspect of your life experience, because it adds to the maturing of character, will also add to the range and deepening of your listening, and help you to become ever more alert, aware, attuned and attentive. In the fullness of time, no life experience is wasted. The ultimate purpose and possible use of some events and experiences can only be viewed, and to some extent understood, many years later.

Relating to the whole person

Slow to chide, and swift to bless.

H. F. Lyte's hymn, 'Praise my soul, the King of heaven'

From a steady stance, and an attitude of non-judgemental, benign regard, the listener seeks to understand the whole person: strengths and limitations; values and hidden motives; the shape and direction of their life, past and future. The future direction may be within the speaker's conscious awareness or it may be still in the realm of potential, yet to be perceived and revealed.

The speaker, feeling understood, becomes more self-accepting: this tends to yield creative change. It is only by being more self-observant, more aware of how you are now, that you build a secure base for growth, change, movement. Clearer, wider, more-alert self-observing is the precursor of lasting change.

Listening and responding to the whole person entails attending not only to the what – of experiences such as suffering – but also, indeed especially, to the who, how and why. Who is this unique individual? How are they, in their own way, experiencing pain or difficulty? Respond as much, or more, to feelings as to factual material and overt content.

Tap in to your intuition, and preserve Christ as your model and your inspiration. He could see and read the inner person. He knew the thoughts of others (Matthew 9:4; 12:25). He 'knew what was in man' (John 2:25).

Qualities and Stance of a Skilled Listener

Some core qualities found in those suited to a listening role (whether formal or informal, frequent or infrequent) include:

- A vocation to encourage: literally, 'to give heart'

- Being someone with whom people can feel safe to share their vulnerability

- Unselfishness, putting all of one's energy and focus at the disposal of the speaker

- Wealth of experience of life, resulting in not being easily embarrassed. The wider your experience, the more readily you can find points of contact with, and empathy for, other people

- Warmth of personality

- Genuine interest in others

- Consistency, so far as possible, of receptiveness and emotional tone

- Reliability, in keeping to practical arrangements

- Trustworthy as regards confidentiality – especially because some people are looking for a first person to whom to disclose tender feelings

- Patience, bearing in mind that trust may take weeks or months to build up

- Self-knowledge

- Imagination, which aids empathy, and also helps the feel for personal potential

- Powers of concentration, and the ability to give undivided attention, requiring relative lack of mental chatter and a temporary detachment from one's own concerns

- Knowing one's limits, and when a person may need to be referred to specialist help

- Delight in language, and in the resonance that specific words or phrases have for each person, based on the personal recollections and associations which particular words and phrases evoke

- Memory – this shows the quality of the listener's attention and the extent of their retentiveness; enables them to work effectively with the speaker in tracing the roots and causes of problems, and in making links in thought patterns and/or behaviour patterns; and helps explain why someone is suffering greatly – when a current difficulty or emotional pain reawakens a previous experience, thus causing a double trial

Looking at this (preliminary) list, and keeping in mind that good listeners score quite well on most of these items, we may conclude that good listening is no small undertaking.

Not looked at item by item, listening is not about doing special things, but rather assisting other people to feel unique, more special, to an appropriate and healthy degree, in their own eyes and estimation.

I was talking recently with a colleague, and we came to the question of what we would look for in an ideal listener. From her analyst, my friend had needed and found three qualities: safety, attention and meaning. And the vital first of these is safety or security.[10]

Safety

Nothing is more precious for health of relationship than trust. For an intimate sharing of one's privacy – regrets, shame, hopes – there has to be an assurance of confidentiality, as in the confessional.

Inner pain comes in various forms: unmet needs (practical or emotional), hurtful memories, grief, guilt, regret and remorse, fear or frustration, anger, anxiety, insecurity, fear of rejection, shallow sense of identity, low self-esteem.

Inner pain often tends to make a person feel isolated. This feeling of isolation may come from one or more of several possible causes, such as hiding a family secret, as sometimes happens when one member is an alcoholic or abusive; fearing one will not be understood; imagining that one's worries are rather unusual; not wanting to burden friends; feeling unsure whether one could cope, should long-buried feelings, such as bitterness, come to the surface.

If a person in a state such as this – and with doubts about whether anything constructive could be done by talking with someone about hurts or needs – does find a secure setting, a safe and trustworthy listener who gives attention, and if one has an instinctive feeling that this may be the right time in one's life to open up and seek both healing and meaning, then the relief and release can be profound – even before significant sharing or catharsis have begun.

---

[10] Editor's note: just the first two areas (safety and attention) are explored.

Attention and acceptance

> It has been well said that heart speaks to heart, whereas language only speaks to the ears.
>
> St Francis de Sales, Letter to the Archbishop of Bourges, 5 X 1604.[11]

Nothing opens the mind and warms the heart more than deep and devoted attention. And the listener's quality of attention will encourage, and be a model for, similar depth of attention in the speaker's own self-listening, leading to more awareness of, and more respect for, his own feelings, thoughts and self-expression.

The speaker becomes more present to himself. With more self-knowledge, he gains in confidence to find, marshal and use creatively, the strength of his own resources. Telling his story, and finding it accepted, strengthens his sense of self. Being accepted by another leads to accepting oneself. Self-observation brings change and growth – the cohering of one's identity.

To give of your time to a person is to affirm that person's worth. And to go on giving of your time helps to overcome the deep-rooted fear of rejection which is one of the main features of insecurity.

If the speaker experiences a relationship in which someone believes in them and in their value and individuality, their self-esteem rises. To be accepted unconditionally, and to be respected and understood, is therapeutic, relaxing, freeing: the speaker feels free to be and express their true self.

Emerson's aphorism about the nature of friendship applies also to a sensitive listener: 'a person with whom I may be sincere. Before him I may think aloud' ('Friendship', *Essays*).

---

[11] Sisters of the Visitation (ed.), *St Francis de Sales in his Letters* (London: Sands & Co, 1954).

Much of the relaxation in an affirming relationship comes from not having to waste energy: in putting on a good, brave, cheerful appearance, or in hiding uncomfortable feelings or memories, or in masking less-attractive parts of one's past or personality.

The speaker then does not have to adapt or bend to the listener's expectations. Thus all energy can be used creatively, constructively. Individuality can emerge and declare itself. Self-awareness increases. Stuck and negative patterns are unblocked. Freedom of choice expands.

To be given time, and to be with a listener who values his own time, often helps the speaker to find more worth in time, in life and in self.

> We mark with light in the memory the few interviews we have had, in the dreary years of routine and sin, with souls that made our souls wiser; that spoke what we thought; that told us what we know; that gave us leave to be what we inly were.
>
> Emerson, *Divinity School Address*, 1839

Right distance heals

A key aspect to feeling accepted unconditionally stems from the listener's careful observing and constant adjusting of distance in the relationship.

Many people who are in need have been adversely conditioned by one parent or both, because the adult-to-child distancing was awry: either too close or too distant, or unstable, fluctuating unpredictably from one extreme to another.

This may result in the speaker's having difficulty in assessing and achieving right distance in friendships. Usually at the extremes of behaviour, they tend either to be clinging or withdrawn and cool.

This new and healing experience of the listener's appropriate distance can yield real and lasting change: giving the speaker the space and the freedom to find and be themselves; and also giving them a new model for better distancing in all their relationships.

Empathy and compassion

I sat where they sat ...

Ezekiel 3:15 (KJV)

Empathy is an essential ingredient of all good listening. The word 'compassion' comes from the Latin for 'have fellow feeling'. You can suffer with or alongside someone else only if you are in touch with, and constantly working on, your own hurts and limitations and vulnerability.

To be related to, and comfortable with, your vulnerability is one of the marks of true humanity, and is an indispensable aid to the creative imagination when faced with another person's pain, giving, as it does, some degree of fellow feeling for what is being experienced. Concentration and memory are much heightened by compassion.

As Jung said, only the wounded healer heals. Jung emphasised the need for the analyst – and this speaks to all in the caring professions – to willingly undertake self-work, and to be ever open to learning from client, encounter and relationship. Empathy and compassion necessitate such self-entering. A listener who is both able and humble will be a constantly developing wounded healer. And some of that development, change and growth will owe its stimulus and impetus to the listener's work and sessions with clients.

The more you accept – deeply and genuinely accept – your own suffering, the more your compassion will increase. And if you really learn from your sufferings, you will grow more insight, more courage and power of endurance, and you will make gains and advance in general creativity.

Stillness

The best listening is unhurried and – if you have faith, and a sense of companionship with God – prayerful. The listener's steadiness brings to the speaker those core human needs of continuity, belonging and being valued.

An unhurried approach enables your concentration to be simultaneously alert and with a relaxed, hovering quality. *Tranquillity is the secret of insight.* The more poised and still you are – in body, in mind, in emotions – the more you will be a source and channel of health and healing. You will be more observant of the other person, of yourself and of what is going on between you. And your stillness will help you assess the timing, the content and the weight of your responses, verbal and non-verbal.

I recall a cellist at a masterclass asking how to produce and sustain a true *pianissimo*.[12] In response and spontaneity, the professor spread out her arms and said simply, *'Pianissimo* is so wide. In order to select the exact choice of vibrato and dynamic weight, you have a large, almost infinite, spectrum to quarry.'

Jane Bown, for many years one of Britain's best portrait photographers, was asked, 'What is the most important aspect of your work, which gives it such high and consistent quality?' The questioner expected one of a range of possible replies, such as originality, technical skills or an instinctive perception and feel for individual human character and characteristics.

Jane Bown gave an unexpected one-word answer: 'Stillness.'

Their strength is to sit still.

Isaiah 30:7 (KJV)

If I could ask God for five gifts as a listener, 'stillness' would be among them. And the others? Gentleness, self-

---

[12] Very quiet.

knowledge leading to continuous self-awareness, and humility. And the greatest of these is humility.

Humility: yielding results to God

The listener's sincerity depends on his not dwelling on, nor trying to measure, the good he may do. His self-awareness and his humility in the face of the mystery of human life, about which we know so much and yet so little, will tell him that his own contribution to another person's well-being is beyond measure.

So much will happen to the speaker, after they finally part, of which the listener may never hear. And he will never know the proportioning of how much he may have done and how much came from the speaker's own newly released resources.

If he has faith, the listener will see all-loving intention, all-empowering, all-good works, as propelled by the hand of God. The whole of life is from Him, and for Him.

> Yet God my King is from old,
> working salvation in the midst of the earth.

> Psalm 74:12

Sacrificial

> Jesus has many lovers of the heavenly Kingdom,
> but few bearers of His Cross.

> Thomas à Kempis, *The Imitation of Christ*

At the heart of all forms of service is a high degree of sacrifice and self-effacing. It is helpful to remember that the word 'sacrifice' comes from the Latin 'make holy'. Listening is sacrificial because it entails humility and self-denial: the self-discipline to moderate what one says about oneself so that the speaker retains the main focus of attention and consideration; the devoting of all energy and faculties for the worth and welfare of the other person. The purpose of the self-denial is positive in intention: to be life bringing.

Bear one another's burdens ...

Galatians 6:2

The more you are actively engaged in the lifelong work of maturing, the more able you are to participate in and accompany the growth and development of another person: participating, yet giving them the freedom to *be*, and the time and space to become their true self.

When you, the listener, are sure of your identity, secure in your separateness, you are, as the French say, comfortable in your own skin. You are not afraid of self-loss, of losing contact with the core of your being. You can therefore endure anger and hostility and challenge without feeling punctured by the powerful feelings of another person. You will not be unduly wary of their fears, tears or desperation. Nor will you be flattered and puffed up by their temporary dependence and need. Rooted in yourself, aware of your own feelings and reactions, you can reach out and enter, as a guest, the speaker's inner world.

In his modest, self-denying stance, a listener eschews the modern values of ambition, competition, reward and tangible results, quickly achieved and measurable (however valuable these may be in their proper sphere).

The listener's service may be given on a voluntary basis. They are not eager for results, and definitely not for quick results. They may have hopes for healing and change in the speaker, but they are hopes, not expectations, and they are gently held, unpressured, non-demanding.

The good listener renounces ownership of change, or of results that may come in the other person's life, personality or behaviour pattern. And the listener is aware of their own needs, and of all that other people give to them.

Oneness

In the art of listening, many of the Christian virtues may be found and developed: patience, moderation and modesty, self-restraint, gentleness, loving-kindness, the giving of peace, the restoring of harmony.

An enriching encounter is based on openness and cooperation. A good relationship creates physical energy and gives psychological strength. In turn, this stimulation generates an attuning to wider vistas revealed by instinct, intuition and the wisdom of the unconscious.

If there is trust, and if a working partnership is strong, then, by the dynamic process of mutual induction, two people become more than the sum of their separate parts and individual qualities. For the listener, it is healing to develop and make manifest human qualities. And to be in the presence of God-given virtues is healing for the speaker. In this spirit, and mindful of everyone's need of more growth towards wholeness, listener can meet speaker as brother or sister in God, not as the superior or as the sole benefactor.

I recall a woman who used to say, 'On Mondays I do my little bit of social work.' Each Monday a young social worker visited my friend, attended to her needs, and was given a cup of tea and few minutes of respite before the hard week to come. Thus were the roles blurred, between visitor and visited, helper and helped.

To think in terms of helper and helped, giver and recipient, is to make an artificial distinction, a false duality. The listener encourages the speaker to do more self-listening; the speaker and the encounter stimulate the listener to do more self-learning. And the speaker – in the revealing of their vulnerability and the exploring of their humanity – speaks for both people. What is most personal is also most universal.

Self-disclosure and the unfolding and growth of personality have a sacramental quality. Real and mutually rewarding relating is two people trusting each other and learning from each other, often in unexpected ways. In real relating, the uniqueness of each person is preserved within a joint endeavour.

True oneness, healthy oneness, does not mean fusion. Nothing is more destructive of relationship (in any form) than psychic fusion. A couple who are in harmony, and share affection, are *as* one, yet they remain two.

Love

> The other one and I, and we together, in this moment in this place, are a unique, unrepeatable occasion, calling for a unique, unrepeatable act of uniting love. If this call is not heard by listening love, if it is not obeyed by the creative genius of love, injustice is done.[13]

Because we cannot feel affection for everyone, love does not necessarily imply liking. But love can evoke and inspire the loving of the less attractive into loveableness.

Love and listening are linked in many ways. Love aids depth of understanding.

Love fosters tolerance, curbs any tendency to be judgemental, and takes one beyond the opposites: good or bad, like or dislike.

Love bridges apparent separateness and superficial differences. Love goes behind and beyond surface appearance.

---

[13] Paul Tillich, *The New Being* (London: University of Nebraska Press, 1955), p. 32.

And so love helps you see potential, and enlarges the frame and scope of your listening.

If they feel rooted in their transcending centre, or soul, the listener finds oneness and reconciliation, where once was division and distrust. Fear narrows; love widens.

Love clarifies and safeguards the motives for what you say, and why you are a listener.

Love facilitates unconditional giving. Love gives without any 'if only': 'If only you will be this. If only you will do that.'

Love, being self-effacing, is always ready to hear and share joys as well as problems, and shows wholehearted delight in the emotional health and total well-being of other people.

In the last analysis, love and goodness are not really given and bestowed by you: they are inspired by God and are channelled through you.

Love strengthens fortitude and forbearance, ensures reliability and trustworthiness, and warms compassion.

Love mobilises hope. This is *the* secret of good listening.

SILENCE

Silence as a Projective Screen

*The eternal silence of these infinite spaces terrifies
me.*

Pascal, Pensées[14]

*

Out of deep silence comes the perfect word.

A Desert Father[15]

At the concert hall of Woodstock, New York, in 1952, pianist David Tudor gave one of the most remarkable performances in the history of music – by not playing a single note. We shall return to what happened at this musical and para-musical event, but first the background.

John Cage, an American composer, was fascinated by silence, even to the point of being shut in a soundproofed room at the Harvard physics laboratory to find out what, if anything, such as his own heartbeat, he could hear. He came to the conclusion that there is no total silence, in nature or in music.

He was inspired to 'compose' a work without musical notes, which he entitled *4'33"*. This refers mainly to time, but also to feet and inches, depicting the space–time continuum. The final impetus came after contemplating the device of a

---

[14] Blaise Pascal, trans. A. J. Krailsheimer, *Pensées* (London: Penguin, 1995).
[15] Benedicta Ward SLG, *The Sayings of the Desert Fathers* (London: Mowbray, 1975).

contemporary artist who, by painting a canvas completely white, intended to show how art is an interaction between the work and the observer. In this example, the only images on the painting were from shadows cast by whatever or whoever was in front of it.

Each of the three movements of *4'33"* was marked by David Tudor by closing and opening the cover of the piano's keyboard. Apart from these brief actions, Tudor sat still, and attentive.

John Cage wanted audiences to become aware, during a piece of music, of the surrounding sounds – outer ones, as well as those in the mind of each listener – that were not directly intended by the composer. When *4'33'* was first played, external sounds included coughs and sneezes of the audience as well as sounds from outside the hall, which was open to woods at the back. The audience could hear the patter of rain on the roof of the hall, and wind gusting through trees.

The inner reactions of the audience were equally loud. In a most unusual way, *4'33"* was keenly listened to. Composer and pianist were subjected to a variety of responses. Some members of the audience muttered in puzzlement. Perhaps David Tudor is unwell? Or is he having a memory lapse?

Some people laughed at what they took to be a musical hoax. Others felt insulted, as if their intelligence had been scorned. Some saw – or heard! – *4'33"* as a snub to centuries of representational art. Other people regarded the whole thing as a non-event; many were not aware when the piece began and ended – did not even realise that a performance had been given.

> An horrid stillness first invades the ear,
> And in that silence we the tempest fear.

John Dryden, *Astraea Redux*

The experience of silence is not always golden. How strongly – and, usually, how darkly – we project on to silence. Just as John Cage had observed the way an all-white painting emphasises shadows, so his own *4'33"* brought a mostly hostile and confused reaction. At least initially. Far from being viewed as a non-event, his piece now features in many textbooks and encyclopaedias.

Here we can observe two frequent patterns: the first response to silence is often reluctant. But there is eventually a subtle shift in projection from negative to positive. We shall find another example of this when we come to discuss in more detail the subject of silence and music.

We may note, in passing, how a client tends to change their view of their symptoms. On starting therapy, the symptoms are often seen as wholly negative, to be got rid of. In hindsight, symptoms can be perceived as prompters of inner work, and as carrying a symbolic message which, if heeded, can lead to a freer future.

We find the same negative-to-positive shift in relation to silence, when we look at a typical pattern in friendship. At first, silence feels awkward, a gap that has to be quickly filled. In time, silence brings a new and deeper dimension to the relationship and is not just tolerated, but welcomed. As Metropolitan Anthony of Sourozh said, 'You will not really know another person until you know and understand his silence.' Rilke, in a letter to Paula Modersohn-Becker (12 ii 1902) concurs: 'I hold this to be the highest bond between two people: that each protects the solitude of the other.'

Archetype

There are two kinds of truths. To the one kind belong statements so simple and clear that the opposite assertion obviously could not be defended. The other kind, the so-called 'deep truths', are statements in which the opposite also contains deep truth.[16]

This aphorism about deep truth could also be a perfect description of archetypes, of which silence is one of the supreme. Silence, like all the great and universal human experiences – love, suffering, personal and collective challenges, self-growth – tends to be perceived in a polarised way: either as a gift or a threat. Thus we have John Cage's mother describing *4'33"*, at its first performance, as being like a prayer. Here is a dichotomy. Prayer or non-event? Silence, Janus-like, has, front and back, two faces. Archetypes respect the mysteries of human life and, by including the whole range of possible experience, they speak to every person and can cause and take all kinds of projections.

Collective influences on our attitude to silence

A client's use and experience of silence in therapy has four main components: collective influences; what happens in the therapeutic encounter and process; his conditioning from home of origin, school, work, social and own home life; and the therapist's style and background.

Collective influences on our attitude to silence include the following: negative associations attributed to it by society, and the effects of population growth, noise and the media. Some of these influences arose during the twentieth century.

Silence has associations with the difficulties of those who are on the autistic spectrum; with sulking and withdrawal and embarrassment; with loss of hope, loneliness and night-fears; with solitary confinement and interrogation techniques; with a sense of inner emptiness or void; with being rejected; with sickness and death.

---

[16] Niels Bohr, 'Discussions with Einstein on Epistemological Problems in Atomic Physics' in *Albert Einstein: Philosopher–Scientist* (Cambridge University Press, 1949), p. 66.

There are a number of social situations in which silence is uncomfortable, such as the awkwardness felt towards silence during the early stages of a relationship, of whatever form.

Another example which we all know from experience is the frustration of waiting for someone who is late for an appointment. What bleak thoughts, what wild feelings, erupt into that slow, jilted silence? Hurts, resentment and anger; self-doubts and doubts about the relationship; echoes of being let down in the past, by this person and/or others. On such occasions, positive feelings are usually overpowered by negative ones.

> There can be nothing more opposite to the natural
> will of people than silent waiting.[17]

---

[17] Robert Barclay, *An Apology for the True Christian Divinity* (London: T. Sowle Raylton and Luke Hinde, 1736), p. 353.

Assault on Silence

Population

> *Physical noise, mental noise, and the noise of desire –*
> *we hold history's worst record for all of them. And no*
> *wonder, for all the resources of our most miraculous*
> *technology have been thrown into the current assault*
> *against silence.*
>
> *Aldous Huxley, On Silence (1946)*

Population growth and overcrowding in inner cities have many effects inimical to the pauses in daily life that are needed for attention to silence and one's inner self. There is now more competitiveness for basic needs and an ever-increasing pace of life; hence a demand for fast travel, fast food and fast entertainment. As Douglas Adams once said, 'The darker it gets, the faster we drive.'[18]

Mass tourism within and between countries, and the needs of refugees and immigrants, cause practical and psychological challenges of adjustment – for residents as well as for visitors and new arrivals.

The diminishing of individual physical space has its counterpart in a reduction of inner space: outer and inner space are being crowded out at a perilous rate. City dwellers are in constant danger of losing the balance and rhythm between

---

[18] Douglas Adams and Mark Cawardine, *Last Chance to See* (London: Arrow Books, 2009).

activity and resting – so much so, that tense people pay to be taught how to relax, especially in Western society, which rewards activism and encourages extroversion.

Noise

As well as, and linked to, the pressures of overcrowding are the violence and noise in city life: the relentless din of muzak, of planes, traffic, trains, machines, road drills, sirens and alarms in cars and shops. There is now an expanding industry in noise-reducing technology. Environmentalists speak not only of pollution of air and soil and water, but also of noise pollution. Background sound and noise cause sensory overload and prevent concentration and clear thinking. This contributes to self-alienation, as each person's inner life and space are invaded, and the capacity to enjoy and experience silence is eroded. There is less real listening, both to self and others.

Media

With a proliferation of electronic (now handheld) devices, music and words broadcast from the media are often being used as mere distractions, and therefore evoke no personal response and bring no lasting fulfilment. Music – any music – now permeates taxis, lifts, supermarket aisles, even waiting time on the telephone. Often this music is not even noticed, let alone listened to, leading to an impoverishment of our capacity to attend to music, words and silence.

Just as political and other events are now stage managed for the media, and thereby lose specific quality, so also words – if over-planned, if scarcely listened to, if they are only sound bites causing and pandering to short attention span – may lose impact and weight, uniqueness and memorability.

The television critic of a British national newspaper recently admitted that, having watched more than 500 interviews on one regular programme, he could now recall little or nothing of what anyone – including many famous and eminent people – had said.

The daily broadcast of worldwide human need impinges on man's unconscious as well as on his conscious thoughts and feelings, and he feels powerless to respond, emotionally or practically.

Saturated by opinions and news (often of disasters, and as they are happening) in this age of global communications, the mind has less time and space to focus on inner life, or to absorb and digest daily experiences. Inner discords are being disregarded because of so much outer sound, and preoccupation with externals. Outer listening can become addictive, a defence and an insulation, a running-away from facing oneself. Tensions arise and grow within, but, being covered over, are not adequately perceived or worked on. This defensive flight becomes self-perpetuating, thus increasing individual haste and tension.

Overcrowding, noise, the media, the pace of life and the rapidity of change, social and technological. Man is not keeping up. The mind cannot assimilate this sensory overload and all these pressures: first, because of their number, scale and simultaneous occurrence; second, because each of them requires extroversion. This one-sidedness has dangerous implications in hindering personal integration, especially of the shadow side, eruptions of which in the twentieth century have scarred life at every level: in the home, in the community, in the nation and between nations.

Words/sounds and silence are complementary. Thus the loss of weight of the word, amid the din and the mass and blur of the pervasive media, contributes to our becoming remote from, and even afraid of, silence.

Silence is being pushed to the margins: something to be experienced only by those who sail, ski or climb, or go to a monastery for a weekend retreat. So far behind have we left the everyday experience of silence that we regard it as rare, even unattainable.

Even in the communal worship of some churches, natural custodians of the value and the archetype of silence, we find a distancing. On many a Sunday, worthy intercessions will be offered, but often the priest or layperson leaves – between, 'Let us pray for ... and for ...' – no pause for silent prayer. This is talking prayer, not the prayer of dialogue, of a dialectic between words and listening and silence.

The Cage work had a prophetic message. Because both the audience and the presenters and performers in the media feel awkward and embarrassed by even a few seconds of silence, the archetype of silence is being eroded. Also eroded, in consequence, are tolerance of inner silence as well as of gaps and silences in conversation.

It is interesting to note that, at a time when individual experience of silence is being curtailed, collective use is being made of the symbolism of silence. Thus, politicians and commentators talk about 'the silent majority', and famine-relief workers in the developing world warn of 'a silent emergency'. An archetype may be temporarily neglected, but will eventually resurface, sometimes in a new guise.

Fear of silence

> It is a strange life for you to come to be silent: you
> must come into a new world.
>
> George Fox[19]

Silence ruffles, disturbs and challenges our surface patterns of thought and behaviour. When entering and encountering silence, many people feel vulnerable, fearing a loss of all that

---

[19] George Fox (ed.), Marcus T. C. Gould, *Gospel Truth Demonstrated*, Vol. 1 (New York: Isaac T. Hopper, 1831), p. 132.

they usually identify with, such as words and striving and the experience of the senses. This is at first daunting and demanding, because it means leaving the familiar world of opinions and everyday activities for the less-known territory of attitudes, feelings, moods and memories. It means a temporary leaving of the ambitious, competitive ego in favour of a trusting dialogue with whatever, if anything, emerges. It means a temporary loss of contact with the outer, surface self; but with the potential for finding the deeper self, the full identity, in silence.

We do not know beforehand what will be the tone or colouring or content of any one experience of silence. We feel exposed and at risk, in the need to learn a new language and a new way of self-relating. As with all new learning, the first stages are among the most difficult.

Encountering silence is more about *being* than *doing*. Experiences and results will vary from one day to the next, and solid gains will come only in the long term. All this is contrary to the expectations most of us have in this era of instant aural and visual gratification.

Nowadays we usually ask in advance, 'What use will this be to me?' But any single experience of silence offers no guarantee that it will be benign or user friendly. Contrary to our conscious willing and ambitions, experiencing silence is a going-into, with no planned or specific object-to-be-sought; and an entering into a new and different time frame. Silence is real but also somewhat intangible and elusive: experiences and results, if any, cannot be assured, predictable or constant.

By simplifying conscious thought, meeting silence is a deliberate opening of oneself to the unknown and the unexpected, a letting-go and an act of faith in an age of plans and forecasts and risk assessments. In and by silence, as we gradually learn its grammar and vocabulary, our perception and experience of silence can move from wariness to welcome, or to a position of hovering between the two.

The Nature and Value of Silence

*Love silence, even in the mind; for thoughts are to
that, as words to the body, troublesome: much
speaking, as much thinking, spends; and in many
thoughts, as well as words, there is sin. True silence
is the rest of the mind, and is to the spirit, what sleep
is to the body, nourishment and refreshment. It is a
great virtue, it covers folly, keeps secrets, avoids
disputes, and prevents sin.*[20]

Silence is far more than merely an absence of words, sounds or
noise, just as peace is more than the opposite of discord or
discomfort. Peace and silence – each exists in its own right, as a
positive and dynamic personal state.

Things arise, grow, in silence: bread in the oven, seeds in
the ground, an embryo in a womb, intuition and ideas and
inspiration in the mind. Silence is the source and ground
(infinite in depth) of hope and creation, and a place for a new
start. Silence is active, just as listening is. Aldous Huxley wrote
of putting oneself into 'a state of alert passivity, of dynamic
relaxation'.[21]

Silence, in its positive mode, is the prime source and
language of balance and truth and healing; of rising above and
transcending some of life's frustrations and irritations; and, by
quietening distractions, of self-knowing and self-discovery,

---

[20] William Penn, *Fruits of a Father's Love: Being the Advice of William Penn to his
Children* (London: James Phillips, 1793), p. 25, XXVII.
[21] Aldous Huxley, *The Art of Seeing* (London: Chatto and Windus, 1964).

giving space at last for 'the moving about of great, secret truths' (F. Scott Fitzgerald).

Silence aids self-honesty. For example, in the recollectedness of silence, one may be able to see afresh one's degree of responsibility in some recent or long-past event.

Silence causes fear because it compels us to go beneath the false self. In silence we face strengths and limitations; conscience, regret and guilt; suppressed hurts and other unconscious material; frustrations and any other concerns about current lifestyle. In silence we see reality more clearly, both within oneself and in one's life. And silence helps coordination: of body and mind, intellect and instincts, and the conscious and the repressed (e.g. fear or shame). To consider exploring the self in silence may seem a risk to the ego (the managing part of the psyche), but the experiencing of silence can result in finding one's true and full identity.

Silence deepens awareness of both self and others. In silence we gain perspective and find our true purpose and priorities, values and direction. This is why silence is both desired and feared: silence assists freedom, freedom gives choice, and choice means responsibility.

When we experience deep silence and are at peace in mind and emotions, we can see widely. Silence brings an expanded view of time and unites our perception of past, present and future. Silence seems to slow the passing of time, and gives pause for both vertical and horizontal thinking. Not only do we explore silence; silence explores us, and teaches.

Silence has many paradoxes. In the aloneness of silence we can sometimes clarify decisions and conduct, see relationships with more objectivity, and gain new perspective on events and aspects and aspirations of outer life.

Silence, by giving a stronger foundation for daily life, can increase our powers of endurance, but to persevere in silence itself needs endurance. Silence is simple and near (even if we do not always make use of its availability), yet it is mysterious. Silence can feel disturbing or peaceful: it can unearth repressed unconscious material as well as give glimpses of the numinous. To enter and encounter silence needs a certain awe, and the experience increases that awe.

There are various differences between solitary silence and a shared silence, each of which has its value. When silence is shared, one's loneliness is shared. This uniting factor can assist in the regaining of hope, and the presence of the other person (or group of people) can be upholding and strengthening, giving courage to persevere in the silence and learn from it, with the assurance, as in psychotherapy, that whatever emerges, however disturbing, can be worked through jointly.

When there is not enough inner listening, a person is liable to be tripped up by his unconscious. 'The world is too much with us,' Wordsworth wrote, in his poem of that same title. Silence brings harmony, and from harmony comes a new sense of proportion, more self-knowing, as well as more awareness of the deeper aspects of other people.

Silence fosters both the intensity of depth and a wider-ranging vision, enabling one to see the essence of things, to make new connections, and to think more in terms of both/and rather than either/or, thus making one inclusive and open rather than suspicious and rejecting. Surface differences and (seeming) contradictions are seen in clearer perspective.

Experiencing and learning from silence cannot be 'done' or rushed; there is no set time frame, no neat programme or solution. A relationship with silence evolves, and needs trust and patience. In silence, one can shed the urge to get and grasp: one can simply be. But simple is not at all the same as easy.

Silence unifies and integrates. This has been verified by research studies which show that, in the relative silence of prayer and contemplation, when the mind is calm and breathing is steady and slow, the two hemispheres of the brain – the left side (logical, linear) and the right (intuitive) – work in closer cooperation, leading to whole-brain perception.

Thus does silence, by widening and uniting one's self, offer the arena and potential for a profound effect, reducing tension and restlessness in body, mind and emotions. In stillness, one can gradually and eventually find and strengthen one's psychological and spiritual centre.

Words that arise from silence

> As words must be learned by listening, and by painful attempts at imitation of a native speaker, so silences must be acquired by a delicate openness to them. Silence has its rhythms and expressions and inflections; its durations and pitches, and times to be and not to be.[22]

Confucius compared language to a wheel, which is made of both spokes and spaces. If this is true of conversation, how much more so of clients in psychotherapy whose speech is inflected by hesitations: the pause amid paradox, the pause of search, of obscurity and confusion, the pause before reaching for new insights.

The value and quality of words spring from, depend on and are nourished by the amount of surrounding silence from which the words come. Words that arise out of silence have more weight. Thomas Kelly has written about this: 'Words, should not break the silence, but continue it … for then silence and words have been of one texture, one piece.'[23]

Silence has a winnowing function, separating carefully chosen words from mere words. In excess, words become weightless and lose their density – for both speaker and listener. If someone who is speaking becomes too caught up

---

[22] Ivan Illich, 'The Eloquence of Silence' in *Celebration of Awareness* (London: Marion Boyars, 1971), chapter four.

[23] Thomas Kelly, *The Gathered Meeting*. Available at http://www.tractassociation.org/tracts/the-gathered-meeting/ (accessed 20th April 2017).

with words, they lose their watchfulness: of self and of their speech, of the other person, and of the other person's response.

Some people blurt out and spout words. Other people listen to their own potential words and truly select them: these words proceed from, and return to, this person's deeper self. At real depth of self-listening, words seem not selected but given, and we are surprised by originality of both vocabulary and ideas.

When we are true to silence, right speech comes. It is only when we pause that what we have just said or are about to say is given clarity and focus – for ourselves and others. Only when we pause is there a real reciprocity between words and silence. As Yeats observed, the 'mind moves upon silence'.[24]

Silence has a paradoxical quality. Often stereotyped as passive, silence can have an active, living tone. Conversely, empty words can be passive and emptily silent, and may say much less than true silence does.

> The silence often of pure innocence
> Persuades when speaking fails

> Shakespeare, *The Winter's Tale*, II ii

Thus it is not only silence that can be silent. In some instances, words may indicate a retreat from communication, such as in (clinical) resistance when a client 'floods' the therapist with bland words, often on surface subjects. This is a hiding, fugitive silence rather than a seeking, searching silence.

Some events and periods of one's life are so deep and poignant that words cannot describe them, especially during and immediately after the initial impact. Just as deeds are said to speak louder than words, so can silence speak louder than words. Conversely, a gust of words which convey no real outreach to another person may be a way of saying, 'I want to

---

[24] Yeats, 'Long-legged Fly' in *The Collected Works of W. B. Yeats: Volume I: The Poems* (New York: Scribner, 1989).

keep you at a distance.' Thus, in an ultimate sense, true speech (that is to say, true communication) is by no means entirely dependent upon words.

On his arrival in Venice as Patriarch, the man who was to be Pope John XXIII said, 'I will try, quickly and silently, to be in touch with all of you.' In October 1962, in his welcome to non-Catholic observers to Vatican Council II, Pope John said, 'Read my heart. You will find more there than in my words.'

Remembering this, a therapist (or a priest or spiritual director) can move from preoccupation with *doing* to the courage to *be*, and to a new valuing of what he gives by his whole attention and his well-centred presence.

Completeness of attention is to listen simultaneously to words and the underlying silence: to be an attentive listening speaker. The more you are related to the central core of your being, which has a surrounding area of silence, the more your words will emerge from creative depths. These words will arise more slowly, and you will, as it were, hear them – at pre-spoken stages – more loudly. With this degree of awareness, you can more effectively decide whether or not it is appropriate to speak those words at all. And if you do choose to speak, your words are more likely to be relatively free of the need to prove yourself and more matched to the current mood, state and needs of the other person.

Silence and the Arts: Paradigm for Psychotherapy

Imagery can help to express and make vivid the elusive ways of the psyche. For example, music and psychotherapy have as ingredients discord and harmony, resolution, inner voices, the importance of rhythm, and the need for what musicians call 'a sense of line'. In therapy, this is the briefly describable but demanding task of consistent, careful following of the client's train of thought, emotion, memory and fantasy.

The ways in which the arts use silence can give a heightened understanding of silence in psychotherapy. Both prove that silence is not only a space for solitary self-finding, but also a potential area and atmosphere for cooperation and collaboration.

A well-known actress spoke recently about her part in one of Shakespeare's works: she had found it easier and more freeing to 'play' the silent passages than the scripted ones. One of the marks of great actors is that they know how to use the pauses and silence between words. A leading British director once said, 'It is in the pauses that a theatre audience brings a scene to life.' The concept of the audience as vital participants in the performance of drama – and especially during silences – is almost identical to what can happen in the concert hall.

Beginning and ending with silence

One of the intentions of John Cage for *4'33"* – an intention amply fulfilled – was to show that there are many different types of silence. Each member of the audience filled each phase – just before the start, during the 'performance' and after the end – with different emotional reactions and imaginative responses: different according to the individual and also according to the specific period of time.

Moreover, the type of silence, and the response to it by audience and performers, will vary according to the music. For example, the beginning of Beethoven's Fourth Piano Concerto had a special significance for the composer. The musical convention of his period was to begin a concerto with an orchestral *tutti*. Instead of this, Beethoven allows the pianist – *dolce*, softly and with subtlety – to present the first subject, a *cantabile* theme. As soloist and audience cross the threshold from silence to sound, the crossing is gentle, almost gradual, because the music conveys an extended moment, a mood, of poise and depth and awe.

What a contrast between the quiet expectancy before this concerto and the vibrant silence which precedes a performance of Beethoven's Fifth Symphony, and its throbbing, fate-laden opening motif.

If a musician has a real dedication to his art, he will begin playing, any and every work, from a basis of deeply felt silence and state of recollection. This is the natural latency and reverence that precedes all true beginnings, whatever the activity may be.

At the end of a performance – if there has been real communication between musician(s) and audience – the experience is absorbed into silence before the applause. This response of gratitude from an audience is regarded by unself-seeking musicians as a tribute of greater worth and substance than the ecstatic clapping that sometimes begins a few bars before the end.

Silent awe in a concert audience at the end of a performance, when a musician has conveyed his sense of love for his art, has perhaps a parallel with the weighty, held silence between people after the sharing of a description of pain.

The deepest aesthetic experiences can contain a yearning beauty so moving that we feel it to be almost painful: a 'poignant' beauty means this very quality – a beauty which pierces. And mystics, through all ages and from different cultures and religious traditions, have written of feeling wounded by God's love. One of the most famous locations of this description is in the chapter about the Night of the Spirit in St Teresa of Ávila's *The Interior Castle*.[25]

These reflections about the silence before and after a concert performance serve as a reminder of how crucial are the silences at the start and end of a therapy session, for it is those moments which set the tone and framework for the whole hour. It is in those hour-framing silences that a therapist can give implied assurance that the session and the work as a whole will, in the words of Abraham Maslow, have an atmosphere that is 'receptive, non-interfering, non-demanding, and letting be'.[26]

Joint relating to silence

Some music students, as well as some solo performers who are relatively new to the concert platform, are shy of silence, and they tend to shorten silences in their eagerness to be active. Their embarrassment often stems from a fear of negative projection: during a silence, some members of the audience may momentarily wonder if the soloist has lost their way, owing to faulty memory, or think that they are not sure how to phrase the next passage. Silence feels exposing (to a musician

---

25 St Teresa of Ávila, trans. A Discalced Carmelite, *The Interior Castle* (London: Sands & Co, 1945).
26 *The Farther Reaches of Human Nature* (New York: Arkana, 1984).

or a therapist), just as playing slowly tends to expose every nuance and any error.

But when a musician gains in maturity and poise, they may come to relish and welcome silences, and use them creatively. Both the musician and the audience experience a kind of release during a silence, and build a new bond and confidence in each other, as well as a real joint relatedness, and a deeper one, to the music.

For the performer, this release may, in part, give relative freedom from a preoccupying fear of playing wrong notes. But the feeling of release is more than this: it is a shedding of the last vestiges of self-consciousness and self-display; an opportunity to become more absorbed in the score, and in the moment-by-moment experience of playing; and a chance to develop his powers of listening.

The ultimate aim is for a comprehensive listening, in which the performer is simultaneously aware of all his faculties, bodily and emotional, and of the inner responses of the audience, and of any extra-musical sounds from inside or outside the hall. At the same time as this quality of wide awareness, the performer will show careful application to their instrument, their music making, and their fellow musicians. This is just the sort and degree of multilayered listening which a psychotherapist or good spiritual director seeks to cultivate.

Silences which are closely attended by both performer and audience foster a merging: the listening by the performer, the listening by the audience, and the music, become as one. These moments are intense as well as light: light in the sense of illuminating; and light in the sense of movement, and in-the-moment flexibility of phrasing and expression. The musician can then, in the midst of performance, and immeasurably assisted by the attention and participation of the audience, gain a sudden new insight into the composer's intentions.

With some clients, at some phases of psychotherapy, there can be a form of merging (although the therapist will always preserve a degree of objective detachment) in which it is said that 'unconscious speaks to unconscious', when new and crucial insights and intuitions may occur to either person, or to both – sometimes simultaneously.

The better and more thorough the preparation, the more will security be felt when on the concert platform. The greater the security, which is the result of discipline, the more the scope for spontaneity and inspiration in the moment.

Discipline in combination with spontaneity opens a way for the deepest creative impulses. Psychotherapy too is at its most creative when the therapist's capacity to be surprised frees and enables a client to mobilise imagination and loosen old patterns of thought, emotions and behaviour.

Just as a musician's vitality and freedom during performance is the pinnacle of accumulated hours and years of application, scales, practice and rehearsal, so also a session in which a client gains new insight usually only comes after a long investment of time and energy, emotional and psychic, by both therapist and client. Movement in therapy requires ego strength, perseverance and long reserves of stamina – from both people. For those who have embarked on therapy, regularity of self-work and attendance is fundamental, just as discipline is soil for the buds of artistic imagination, or grace in spiritual life. All of these three endeavours – music, therapy and spiritual life – are rooted and grow in an ever-deepening experience of silence.

The willingness of a performer to be open, and to be ready to be surprised by new experience – this humble and self-sacrificing willingness – has a link with the therapist who comes to each session – and functions within each session – as free as possible of expectation and personal needs.

Varieties of silence in music

> Elected Silence, sing to me
> And beat upon my whorlèd ear,
> Pipe me to pastures still and be
> The music that I care to hear.

Gerald Manley Hopkins, 'The Habit of Perfection'

Silence in music occurs at many different stages of a work, and each stage and its silence has a different feel and quality: between movements, between variations, before and after a *cadenza*, and at the peak of a *crescendo*.

A musician is taught to play the notes in such a way that the music continues – in message, meaning and impact – through a rest, a pause, a silence. The apt use of rests and silence is intrinsic to the life and rhythm of performance, and variations in the use of space within the music's fabric by judicious *rubato* (the subtle use of freedom with time values) prevent monotony, such as when a passage is repeated.

A rest in music is not a vacuum, not just an interval between notes. If a student pushes or rushes through a silence, fudges it, feels embarrassed by it, finds no purpose or potential for expressiveness in it, his teacher may ask a short question with profound implications: 'Did you hear the silence?' Profound, because the more the silences are felt by a performer, the more will he convey in and through sound.

Just as the tone and character of silence in music depend on the placing within a work, so too does the experience of silence in psychotherapy vary according to the stage of the hour. (See later section: 'Silence and the analytic hour').

Learning the Language of Silence

Teach us that silent language which says all things.

Fr Jean-Nicolas Grou, SJ

What we discovered earlier about John Cage, about the Beethoven works, and about a music student's growing awareness of silence, may help in becoming more aware of types of silence in psychotherapy. We need to listen to the language of silence, to its sound, tone and texture, inflections and nuances; to observe the levels and stages of silence; and, above all, the therapist needs to listen to their own experience of silence and to try to sense how the client is experiencing it. Thus, during a silence, the two central questions, one leading on to the other, are: What kind of silence are the therapist and the client experiencing? What is its reason, meaning, purpose, direction?

The second question will be looked at in the chapter 'Silence in Psychotherapy'. As to the first, here is the start of a classification of types:

Positive	Peaceful	Releasing, freeing, liberating
	Harmonious	Restoring, renewing
	Eloquent, speaking	Hopeful
	Creative	Trusting
	Healing	Connected

Negative	Elusive	Empty
	Anxious	Cut off, schizoid
	Awkward	Wary, suspicious
	Dull, bored	Persecuting

Neutral	Absorbing (digesting)	Searching
	Waiting	Hovering
	Transitional	Expectant
	Reflective	Ambivalent (in the literal sense)

General	Positive	Negative
Colour	Vivid	Drab, grey, dark
Weight	Light	Heavy
Distance	Uniting	Withdrawn
Temperature	Warm	Cold
Density	Solid, tangible	Transparent or dense
Animation	Living	Lifeless
Motion	Fluent	Stuck
Relationship	Shared, supported	Judging, rejecting
Attention	Focused, condensed	Distracted, scattered, aimless

Depending on the transference situation, a client may have an overall reaction to silence, feeling it to be hostile and demanding or comforting and reassuring. This reaction may be helpful in assessing the state of the psyche and the stage of the therapy. For example, if silence is felt as desertion, this could indicate regression to the oral level; if felt as pleasant dependence, regression to the introjective level. Or silences may be arising because a client is depressed and is thinking and speaking slowly or in bursts, and thus needs to be with someone who is very patient during intervals between speaking.

Many are the possible quasi-negative causes of, and reasons for, silence during a session. It may indicate uncertainty, a dependency need, or a seeking to find out what the therapist may be wanting or expecting to be said, in form and/or content. Alternatively, the client's silence may signal an angry retaliation against the therapist's silence. Whatever the cause and tone of silence, positive or negative, there will probably be ample material for work within the transference.

Therapists, many of whom have much facility in speech, need daily to recall, by understanding and imagination, that, for some clients, words – both the finding and expressing of them – are hard, even frightening. To speak may entail risk, such as fear of criticism; and to speak with clarity presupposes a relatively secure self-identity.

Often, the deeper and earlier the material that is emerging, the more are space and silences necessary. Conversely, the more the silence – more, in the sense of length and/or intensity – the deeper may be the layers of the psyche that are reached. Thus, much care and caution are needed by the therapist in assessing the length and degree of silence which a client can take, especially when working with someone who is potentially self-destructive. And a client's capacity to tolerate and make use of silence will to some extent depend on the length of gaps between sessions.

Silence for a whole hour, or almost a whole hour, may indicate a hiding of deep shame, rage, fear or thoughts and fantasies about suicide or about violence – to self and/or others. Such a long silence may be pathological, and the reasons for it should be promptly and thoroughly investigated.

If a client says he has 'nothing to say today', this may indicate a general resistance, or it may be a replay of the form of a past event soon to be mentioned.

Silence has an almost infinite variety of shades of tone and feeling. To take but one example, a therapist needs to distinguish with care between an expectant silence that indicates a wait before resuming, perhaps with the client's being on the verge of new insights, in contrast to a pause that invites or hopes for a response.

When learning to read the language of silence in the consulting room, we come to realise that its dictionary is vast, as many-paged as that of sound in any form – verbal, musical or the sounds of nature – and that, although very closely related, the language of silence is harder to learn, and needs even more sensitivity, than the language of words.

Silence in the orientation phase of therapy

In the early stages of working with a client, the therapist should not be too quick to label awkward silences as a sign of incompatibility, or of a fundamental impediment to eventually achieving a satisfactory working alliance. These silences may be part of a general early resistance and/or discontent during the orientation phase: many clients speak of the strangeness of this one-sided relationship, in which all the self-disclosure and most if not all of the main initiatives have to come from only one of the two participants. And the therapist will bear in mind that a client who has difficulty in taking initiative may feel far from being a good, cooperative, acceptable patient in what they at first suppose is only or mainly talking treatment.

Early on, a client's controlled and controlling silence may reflect ambivalence between an urge and a fear about uncovering and exploring intra-psychic material, against which, for so long and with such strong and complex defences, they have guarded, with the investment and sacrifice of much valuable psychic energy.

This fear is not only a fear of the power and of the negative (or dark) parts of the unconscious – in other words, a fear of where silence may lead to – but also a fear that, if the flow of one's words stop, this may entail loss of sense of self. Thus, especially for a person of low self-esteem and fragile ego-strength, silence can be intimidating and even frightening. And this fear may be increased by being in the presence of someone perceived as having insight. In other words, and especially in this early phase of the therapeutic journey, the client may feel that the power base in the consulting room is tilted heavily in favour of the therapist.

Because a client's holding-on to words, clutching at sound, may be a desperate attempt to maintain a sense of self, the therapist will need to discern carefully how much silence the client can tolerate at this stage.

Early on, if working on specific transference implications of silence, the therapist may find it useful or necessary to explain their general use of silence: that it indicates and stems from their own patient waiting, and that the client always retains choice and control over content of material and the timing of its being mentioned.

The therapist may also explain that their relative (or complete) silence on particular occasions, when asked a personal question, is intrinsic to the therapist's neutrality. Although silent in the sense of holding back from self-disclosure, the therapist may be active in suggesting that work be done to find out what projections, fantasies or transference reactions may be associated with a personal question, especially if it is put after the therapist has initially explained the way of working.

Resistance

Any enquiry into silence and psychotherapy needs to take full account of resistance. For, just as a client brings into the consulting room something of the collective wariness about silence, they also bring a personal element.

Fear of silence derives mainly from a fear of facing one's shadow side. Silence entails a self-confronting: facing sad memories, guilt, current worries, concern about the future, thoughts about unwelcome habits and tendencies, self-doubts. A silence entails a look into dark corners of the psyche, as yet unexamined, including primitive instincts. Thus silence is the threshold for the whole agenda of therapy.

My first learning about resistance came with an element of surprise and humour. Our seminar leader, masking the depth of the subject, said, 'Hands up all those who think the client will give you 100% cooperation.' Filled with the desire to bring change and perhaps cure to people in need, most or all of us fell into the trap, and raised our hands. With a wise and wry smile, she said, 'Well, wait and see.'

In a classic dictum, Freud said that resistance will be present at every stage of the analysis, and in every session. Much care is needed to discern the focus of the resistance: how much is owing to fear of facing potentially painful repressed material, and how much to the transference?

The stronger the resistance, the stronger is the transference. The mode of resistance may take various forms, from withdrawal into a defended silence to incessant talking. 'Flooding' may take the form of talking at length about surface topics, reading from long notes written between sessions, or wanting dreams to dominate the material of the session. The purpose in most cases is to ward off a combination of anxiety, transference-hostility (to the therapist and/or the process) and reluctance to embark on deeper exploration into unconscious material: a holding-on to the working alliance rather than a yielding to a transference neurosis.

If the therapist is passive during a retreating silence, they will be colluding with the resistance. On the other hand, they will usually (outwardly) ignore, and certainly not over-investigate, small resistances. They therefore have to let the client feel and fully experience silences, and come to own their resistance, before beginning to offer interpretation. The therapist has to find a middle position: in a silence, they will be alert not aloof, so that the silence (but not the resistance) feels mutual, shared.

Interpretation

How can a therapist assist a client across the quasi-silent threshold from unconscious to conscious? Two models or paradigms may be suggested. One is the Jungian concept of attending at a rebirth, the birth of new consciousness. The other, which is more prosaic in both senses, is to enable the client to, as it were, write their autobiography; this may include myths (in the Jungian sense: meaning cultural patterns, not legends) – personal myths, family myths and/or collective myths.

This assisting, attending and enabling is to be done circumspectly, in an indirect and allusive way, discreet in timing and in manner. The therapist proceeds by way of inference, induction, accumulation of data.

How best to interpret? Less by statement, more by suggestion, and by linking what the client has already manifested by words and/or behaviour: often a combination of conscious verbalising, dream material, transference reactions and acting out (inside and/or outside the consulting room).

Silences may be allowed to lengthen in order to heighten resistance, and thus highlight transference feeling and reactions prior to demonstration, interpretation and working through.

When offering interpretation, I work in stages: reminding the client of various connected manifestations; suggesting an interpretation; and then, if there is recognition by the client, inviting them to reformulate it in their own words. Some clients will then, on their own initiative, add further examples, from our analytic work or from their daily life, or both. This will be a sign of their coming to own the interpretation, and will symbolise it as a joint venture and a shared discovery.

I often return to Jung's *Modern Man in Search of a Soul* to read what he said about interpretation:

> I need not try to prove that my dream interpretation is correct.
>
> The psychotherapist ... must have no fixed ideas as to what is right ... otherwise he takes something from the richness of the experience.
>
> .... it is highly important for the analyst to admit his lack of understanding from time to time, for nothing is more unbearable for the patient than to be always understood. The latter in any case relies too much upon the mysterious insight of the doctor, and, by appealing to his professional vanity, lays a dangerous trap for him. By taking refuge in the doctor's self-confidence and 'profound' understanding, the patient loses all sense of reality, falls into a stubborn transference, and retards the cure.[27]

---

[27] Carl G. Jung, *Modern Man in Search of a Soul* (London: Routledge Classics, 2001), p. 9.

Silence in Psychotherapy

... the very sigh that silence heaves
'I stood tip-toe upon a little hill'.

John Keats

And how the silence surged slowly backward.

Walter de la Mare, 'The Listeners'

Psychotherapy is not only 'talking treatment'; it is also silent treatment. Silence in therapy allows the client time and room to delve into their intra-psychic areas, to clarify thoughts and emotions and values, and, at a deeper level, to recall and work with memories, fantasies and dreams. Silence thus helps in the central therapeutic work of uniting and integrating inner and outer, and conscious with unconscious, so that the client can eventually – to enlist Matthew Arnold ('Sonnet to a Friend') – see life steadily and see it whole.

One of several differences between solitary silence and shared silence is that the presence of another person – after any negative transference reactions to silence have been analysed – can help to mobilise the considerable stamina and emotional staying power that are needed to remain in and with silence, and to have the courage to begin and to continue to learn from whatever arises.

One finds what is right for oneself by listening carefully to one's inner voices, by listening in order to be moulded, guided, directed. The good psychotherapist helps his patient in the same way – by helping the patient hear his drowned-out inner voices, the weak commands of his own nature, on the Spinozistic principle that true freedom consists in accepting and loving the inevitable, the nature of reality.

Similarly, one finds out what is right to do with the world by the same kind of listening to its nature and voices, by being sensitive to its requiredness and suggestions, by hushing so that its voices may be heard.[28]

One of the highest forms of awareness and intelligence is the ability to see connections, to perceive new relationships between things. In silence one can grow in self-understanding through seeing new links: both between parts of one's personality and between various aspects of one's background and current life (such as defence mechanisms).

Silence enables a client to roam in reflection – far from the insistent claims and demands of the present – and think about past and future, and make new connections between the three phases of time.

Many clients, especially in the early stages of therapy, will label silence as unproductive. They think they come mainly, or only, to talk. They may have temporarily lost the sense of linkage between words and silence. Moreover, they may project their own view (that silence in therapy is wasted time) on to the therapist, and assume they will be impatient with silence.

Until the client becomes orientated to the ways and the full potential of therapeutic work, they and the therapist may see

---

[28] Abraham Maslow, *The Farthest Reaches of Human Nature* (New York: Viking, 1971), p. 124.

silence from different angles. The therapist may regard silence as creative, a giving of space; the client may feel silences to be difficult, even to the point of being inhibiting.

This sort of client perspective derives from several possible sources. They may still be getting used to the necessary one-sidedness of the relationship, with no self-disclosure by the therapist and with the client expected to take the main initiatives in choosing material to talk about. Or, in a previous experience of therapy, silences may have been awkwardly handled.

The client may have come from a home-of-origin where they did not learn to use or value silence. In early life they may have been given 'the silent treatment' by a sibling, a peer at school, a parent or another authority figure. A mindset may have been created, associating silence with withdrawal of affection, to which may have been added the uncertainty of not having known how long a period of disapproval might last. Thus negative projection on to silences in the consulting room can be a useful starting point for work on the transference.

In time, to come to know a truly accepting silence can help foster a new and well-founded feeling of self-esteem; and relocate authority within, instead of being over-influenced by and always on the watch for, the moods, opinions and reactions of other people. To have one's silences received with calmness and understanding is a corrective to early learned responses when, to feel acceptable and appreciated, many a client constantly felt forced to behave in certain ways: to placate, explain, apologise, entertain.

Silence creates its own circumscribed space, lessening distractions, lifting awareness away from everyday matters, fostering objectivity and new insights. The Quakers used to speak of silence as having a sifting power. In today's terms, we would say that silence challenges habits of thought, and especially low or false self-image, and encourages the facing, finding and accepting of the real self. Furthermore, the contents of the unconscious, usually feared, may yield new potential for creative living and relating, in addition to repressed memories and aspects of the personality that need to be integrated.

If the atmosphere, in the room and in the silence, has a hovering quality, a freedom to move, this will encourage the emerging of unconscious material, gently nudged by the therapist.

From the base of a trusting, supporting silence, leading to deeper material from the psyche, the client may make more use of primary speech, as they find and articulate what had until then not been consciously formulated. A session in which client and therapist experience and use a deep silence can bring new movement, which months of previous work had not been able to do, or at best had been but a preparation.

A silence such as this has two main beneficial effects. It heightens for the client the effect, impact and meaning of their own words: this can contribute to growth in the sense of self-identity. And new intuitions and insightful connections may occur to client or therapist or both, and sometimes simultaneously, thus enhancing the working alliance.

When a client begins to feel more comfortable with silences during sessions, this is often a result both of new self-assurance and of feeling easier in the analytic relationship. This confirms and reinforces a central feature of personal growth: the clear link between relating to self and relating to others. Movement, change, acceptance and growth within one's self usually has a parallel (in impact and often in simultaneity of time) in relationships.

Silence and the analytic hour

Client

Silence at the start and end of the analytic hour helps to create a framework for whatever emerges during a session. Furthermore, silences at start and end may stem directly from circumstances. At the start, the client may need time for orientation as they try to make a transition, gain focus and screen out external impressions from preceding hours of work and travel. Only then can they reflect and select their material.

A client's use of silence – in frequency and duration – will depend on a number of factors. These include:

- Stage of hour

- Time of day

- Season of year

- Age

- Frequency of sessions

- Psychopathology, ranging from the relatively silent (such as if depressed or schizoid) to the more verbal (such as if manic or hysterical)

- Degree of resistance and its form (such as by 'flooding' the hour and the therapist with material)

- The type of transference

- The counter-transference situation

- The word-silence pattern and resistance pattern of recent sessions

- The stage of the working alliance

- The temperament and style of the therapist

- The personality of the client (such as in the introvert–extrovert spectrum)

- The weight and depth of the material

- The client's stress level (ranging from pressure of speech during catharsis to the deep and often unspeakable mystery of grieving)

Therapist

The therapist will usually be relatively quiet during the first half of a session. Material which might at first seem important may later be seen as resistance, or as prelude to the hour's[29] main content. But the therapist needs to be careful not to make too radical a switch to being more verbal and active during the second half of a session, and should be careful about the timing (and weight) of interventions in relation to the time of the client's departure.

Much sensitivity is needed by a therapist in handling and understanding silences towards the end of a session. For example, if a session is the last before a weekend or a holiday, silence may indicate the client's sorrow and/or anger about separation from the therapist.

Freud's guidance to analysts-in-training was, 'No advice, no reassurance, no self-disclosure'. His injunction against reassurance may at first seem puzzling, but it is based on the wish to save clients from states of undue dependence on their analyst.

The therapist needs to watch and guard against any impulse to offer words of reassurance at the end of a session. By being less active at this stage, they will be implicitly affirming that the client can learn to bear the hurt and frustration of separation, and that the separation will be temporary.

Much care has to be given to avoid underestimating a client's innate hope and courage. Indeed, a basic aim of psychotherapy is to rouse and mobilise these traits. Any reassurance, however well intentioned, fosters and perpetuates

---

[29] Meaning 50 minutes.

dependence. Moreover, reassurance can sound clichéd or even patronising.

The therapist's relative amount of silence towards the end of a session, and near-absolute silence at the door, may be more memorable, more supportive and strengthening than words could be. Such silence may reach a deeper level of the client's psyche, and be felt as a more original gesture.

The therapist's stance

Technique for the use of words – those initiated by the therapist and when responding to the client – is more developed than technique for the use of silence. Both therapist and client need a constantly sought and mutually given space so that each can sense whether words or silences are appropriate at any particular stage of a session, and it is from this basis that each has freedom to move between speaking and reflecting.

The therapist's general stance and guidelines are: to be slow to break a silence; to be alert to the type and meaning of silences; to be clear about timing and purpose whenever beginning to speak, as well as when embarking on investigation of the surface cause and deeper causes of silence; and to try to foresee how the client may see and react, at a conscious and preconscious level, to any form of intervention.

> Do not be in a hurry to fill an empty space with words and embellishments, before it has been filled with a deep interior content.[30]

The therapist's clarity of intent and awareness of their reasons prior to every breaking of silence will help prevent any introduction, however subtle, of their own agenda. In addition,

---

[30] Alexander Elchaninov, *The Diary of a Russian Priest* (St Vladimir's Seminary, 1997).

they will need to distinguish carefully between an active, waiting silence on their part and a passive silence which, if it were to last too long, could be felt by the client as a rejection. A tendency towards a passive stance might indicate a need for the therapist to look for work-blocking counter-transference reactions in themselves. For example, during an aggressive-toned silence on the client's part, the therapist might sense negative-transference feelings and have a fear of post-silence hostility.

Silence is a potent therapeutic instrument. The art of psychotherapy revolves around a balanced, judicious use of silence and words. At times, what is needed is to name, to make explicit. At other times, the wise course is silence: the therapist 'gives' by holding back – for example, by not revealing personal details or opinions, so as to facilitate transference projections; and by delaying an intervention or interpretation until an apt moment.

Formulating the content of an interpretation sometimes comes more readily than knowing or sensing when best to proffer it, or whether to mention it at all. The more secure and experienced a therapist is, the less will their use of interpretation, and their whole approach to interventions of whatever weight, be tainted by a need to bolster their role and own sense of being effective.

One result of a therapist's sense of security is flexibility of technique: a flexibility within and based on their own school of training and its ethical standards.

Various questions arise about the use of silence. Because therapy is primarily an art, the following will have to be kept as live questions, to be answered according to individual style and the needs and capacities of each client:

1. Is silence in a session always valuable? For example, some therapists may wish to be slightly more facilitating of verbal content in the early stages of therapy, because a

client has not yet become orientated to this new type and way of relating.

2. Should a therapist ever break a silence? If so, why? In what circumstances? After how long a silence, and after what type or tone of silence? What should be the form and content of the intervention? Perhaps relatively short, and neutral in weight and direction – not a leading question – so that the client retains the main initiative.

3. Should the therapist break a silence – for example, at the start or finish of a session – so as to raise business matters, such as about payment of fees or days and times of sessions?

4. Should a therapist always allow every session to end in silence?

5. How much eye contact is appropriate during a long silence? An occasional exchange of glances may help indicate to a client that their experience of silence is being shared.

If the therapist is alert during silences, they may notice with more perception and understanding those short but often very significant and poignant moments which point towards a client's inner state: the sigh or hesitation, the pause of inhibition, the wistful look or side glance, or new and greater freedom and relaxation in face or gesture.

During silence, the therapist's own posture and gestures, including the smallest movements of the body, may be noticed and interpreted, and often misread, by a client. For example, if the therapist glances at his watch, this may be taken as a sign of impatience: the client may think the therapist wants the silence to be broken, or the session to finish. Or a look of concentration may be misinterpreted as a frown. Here is much rich material for work with the transference.

Quality of attention

Because deep attentiveness is such a healing factor, and something which many clients may never have been given previously, the therapist needs to maintain a high degree of interior personal silence, so that the attention is free and open. This enables one to be where the client's attention is; and the therapist ensures by self-monitoring that it is the client who is setting the agenda, the pace and the direction.

Attention is founded on inner silence. In order to achieve and maintain this truly silent listening, the therapist needs to screen out any and all obstacles: over-identification with the client's material; personal (as opposed to diagnostic) counter-transference; and extraneous thoughts, feelings or outer distractions.

The relative silence (inner and outer) of the therapist enables them not only to receive and work with what the client is bringing, or by inhibition is not bringing, but also to attend to their own mind and inner being, watching and assessing their own impetus to respond, comment, intervene, interpret, offer a short prompt or ask a follow-up question.

From a silent base, the therapist will be continuously self-evaluating, questioning their motives to speak and watching for traces of inappropriate reactions or of vanity or egoism, and any tendency to offer advice or approval or value judgement, or give a premature or heavy interpretation. The gains from this silent base can include an increase in awareness and responsibility – towards self and others – and a widening of the space to listen to their own intuitions as well as to promptings from the client's unconscious.

Words or silence?

Speech is but broken light upon the depth
Of the unspoken

Source unknown

For ah! We know not what each other says ...
Their sound is but their stir, they speak by silences

Francis Thompson, 'The Hound of Heaven'

When to use words? When to stay with silence? After every session, I review how I handled the hour so that I can learn from it: in a general way, as well as for hoped-for benefit to the work with each particular person. Any flaws in my technique are, nine times out of ten, because of over-activity. As Xenocrates said, 'I have often repented because I spoke, but never have I been sorry that I held my peace.'[31]

My interventions are usually one of four basic kinds. These are, in ascending order of weight: a follow-up question; the gentle underlining of a client's material, intended as empathic mirroring or to highlight a new insight; making a link between material – from within the same session, or from one or more previous ones; a minor or major interpretation.

A formula I now find helpful is this: if I feel that an intervention may be useful, and seems correct both in its form and timing, I will proceed. If I am in any doubt, I rely on silence (or, at most, body language, such as a nod of understanding and/or of encouragement to continue) rather than words.

On the whole I try to allow silence to encourage the next material, rather than relying on prompts by words or gestures. This greater reliance on silence – trusting silence to find its

---

[31] *Val. Max. vii Dict. Fict Memorab 2.*

own direction – is especially important during intense sessions, such as those involving catharsis, grief or the revelation of a secret.

Just as there is a reciprocal relation between silence and words, so also is there reciprocity between a therapist's receptivity – not forcing their own expectations on to the client, even for change and growth – and the client's becoming more centred.

Words have much more weight when they are spoken from, and received by, a silent base: they then emerge from a layer of depth and fullness of meaning and purpose, and with a measured pace. And measured pace and the capacity to pause give poise.

The central issue is not, 'words or silence?' but, 'when are words apt?' and 'when is silence apt?' Socrates said, 'Speak, that I may see you.' We might add, 'You may be silent, so that I may see you – and so that you can see yourself – more deeply.'

From the basis of silence, the client will speak with more gravitas, and will usually notice the way in which their words are being chosen with more economy and more focus. What they say in the consulting room will have impact on them, and this will encourage more reflection between sessions.

Conclusion

There are many layers to the reality of silence. To overcome a fear of silence, and to probe for its meaning, we have to go beyond words, which are at best only partial descriptions, and go on learning from experience.

Psychotherapy, if seen by both the client and the therapist as founded primarily in the soil of silence, moves from surface to depth, from conscious to unconscious, from safety and defence to exploration of the as-yet-unresolved: doubts, memories and hurts.

In addition to all that psychotherapy can offer – from abreaction to reality testing, the developing of social skills and the increase of insight – perhaps one of the most significant and lasting potential gains is seldom mentioned in textbooks, and is rarely one of a client's conscious goals: becoming more comfortable with their inner silence – perhaps for the first time, and perhaps after years of avoidance, such as through over-activity. This in turn may help to reduce a fear of loneliness.

When a person's words and deeper self are not expressed or heard, they shout: with voice or clothing; by actions, which may include violence to self or others; or through their body, as in psychosomatic illnesses.

A central paradox is that by becoming more related to silence, one finds and uses one's full and true voice. This implies a use of primary speech and a gain in spontaneity. A more potent and expressive use of one's voice is symbolic of overcoming passivity and low self-esteem, and of becoming better able to take decisions and take initiatives, in words and in action.

In his famous essay, 'The Capacity to be Alone', Winnicott wrote:

> I am trying to justify the paradox that the capacity to be alone is based on the experience of being alone in the presence of someone ... It is only when alone (that is to say, in the presence of someone) that the infant can discover his personal life.[32]

What Winnicott said about the child's need to learn to be alone and self-contained when with a parent is true also of the repair work that can be done in the consulting room, for an adult who lacked enough of this aspect of early nurturing.

The full significance of a therapeutic relationship, in which silence was experienced, explored and learned from, may not

---

[32] D. W. Winnicott, 'The Capacity to be Alone' (1959) in *The Maturational Processes and the Facilitating Environment* (London: Karnac, 1965), pp. 29-37.

be realised until after termination of the work. The gains in self-awareness, effectiveness and fulfilment can be lifelong.

My analyst's silence had a special depth and relatedness during those central sessions when I was confronting something challenging in my outer and/or inner life. Her giving of a framework of silence was the giving of both space and attention. It also had the qualities of sharing, supporting and understanding. It was a silence beyond words; but if words came from me, hers was a silence ready to receive.

THE HESITANT JOURNEY

The Metaphor of Journey

*Journeys, like artists, are born and not made. A
thousand differing circumstances contribute to them,
few of them willed or determined by the will –
whatever we may think. They flower spontaneously
out of the demands of our natures – and the best of
them lead us not only outwards in space, but inwards
as well. Travel can be one of the most rewarding
forms of introspection.[33]*

Universality

Through all history, in every country and culture, in painting, in
myth and fable and verse, and in real events, journey has been
and is a rich and potent symbol. To Sherpa Tenzing, the first
climbing of Everest, and perhaps the mountain itself, became a
metaphor for the journey of a person's inner life.

In Australia, Aborigines have been on the move, generation
after generation, for thousands of years. Ritual objects – iron,
wood, feathers, stones – are part of a story that belongs to a
portion of the landscape. They do not read stories; they walk
them. If you were to ask, 'How long is your story?' the answer
would not be 'half an hour' but 'two miles'. The adventures,
the history and the teachings of the Aborigines have become
fossilised into rocks, boulders, trees and valleys. At first, a child
learns just their family's stories. By the time the child is old,

---

[33] Lawrence Durrell, 'Towards an Eastern Landfill' in *Bitter Lemons in Cyprus*
(London: Faber and Faber, 2000).

they have become possessor and transmitter of the whole of tribal understanding. Thus, for a people who are always on the move, life is a walk towards wisdom. They are passionate about their land, because the land is their holy book.

In psychotherapy, journey is sometimes a dream symbol for the therapy itself. Jung spoke of the process of individuation as a 'circumambulation of the self'.[34] When we make a physical journey, a pilgrimage, a house move, a change of job, a new start – we ultimately end up back where we started.

The Mountain of God is a prime symbol of revelation and of mystical contemplation. Here Moses saw God in the burning bush. And from the Mountain, a number of great Christian mystics and ascetics derived their illustrations about the ascent to Union with God.

During our reflections on journey, we shall find a recurring theme, which is quintessentially Jungian: the reciprocity between inner and outer life. From this, two axioms are derived. First, inner work and growth lead to outer creativity and effectiveness. Change, lasting change, is from within and grows outwards; and it starts from being, not becoming. Second, some forms of outer life can be attempts to escape from the inner life: this is shown in restlessness, hyperactivity, compulsive shopping, yearly moves of home, for example. It is a frequent delusion that happiness will be found in escape or outer change. Even if you move to a new home thousands of miles away, you still bring with you the same personality, the same conditioning and habits, the same memories, the same unconscious.

Thus, many people have a tendency to be at the mercy of external life. The outer, however appealing, can never calm or fill the void within. Any attempt to change the outer but ignore the inner cannot hope to succeed.

---

[34] *Memories, Dreams and Reflections* (London: Fontana Press, 1995).

Therapy gives a client an experience of developing a closer bond between inner and outer, when memories and repressions are brought to the surface.

Imagery serves where words fail

To describe the ways of the psyche and the unconscious, David Holt, one of my supervisors during my analytic training, used this phrase: 'elusive and yet binding'. In those four words, spoken with an engraved quality, and even a sense of awe and mystery, he encapsulated both the centrality of psyche as well as the difficulty of describing what is happening in the unconscious.

This difficulty is also an opportunity, for two reasons. First, it rouses the therapist to a keener state of alertness. They may – often or usually – take vocabulary and shared language for granted. But nothing better repays attention than to listen to the client as if one were a linguist, an interpreter. Indeed, a skilled therapist may, more than they realise, take account of, and when appropriate adapt to, each client's individual use of language, and even speech patterns. And if the therapist listens carefully, they may detect signs of change when a client switches from *cliché* to more colour, more originality, in the choice of words.

The second benefit that derives from the difficulty of description of psyche is that the client may tend to use image and metaphor, and thus be vivid in expression: vivid to self, and vivid to the therapist. When we are trying to describe the dark or the light of life's experiences – pain, or nature, or the beauty of the fine arts, we instinctively reach for imagery. In our imagery, we often use spatial terms to portray experiences, moods or states of being. Thus we speak of 'the peaks and troughs' of our range of emotions. We 'scale the heights of illumination' or 'fall into the depths of despair'. We are 'up', or we are feeling 'down'.

If I were to think of material from clients, past and present, I recall many phrases that use the metaphor and archetype of journey. Here are a few examples. First the negatives:

- I'm feeling stuck.

- I don't know where I'm going.

- I'm all over the place.

- I'm up in the air.

- I can't see the wood for the trees.

- I can't see the way ahead.

- I'm afraid of going over the edge.

- I keep tripping over myself.

- My partner and I always seem out of step.

The positives include:

- I feel I'm now getting into my stride.

- I'm walking with a lighter step.

- I'm feeling well grounded (or well earthed).

- When we talk, I can now stand my ground.

- I've got a map.

- I know the lie of the land, and can read my compass.

- We're heading in the same direction.

- I know where I'm going.

I offer two observations. One is that both stages of climbing a mountain are hazardous: we 'face an uphill task'; and later, 'everything seems to be going downhill'. We shall briefly return to this topic when we look at the dangers of journey. Second, how helpful these images are. They describe psychopathology. They assist in forming a diagnosis. They mark and signal degrees of change, and what therapists call 'movement'.

It is also worth noting how often a client's description of external events, such as news items, is symbolic of inner life. For example, do they tend to dwell on stories of war and violence? If so, is this perhaps a way of depicting their own anger and struggles?

Mentions of outer journey are sometimes a metaphor for what goes on in the consulting room. There are always three simultaneous journeys: the outer, the inner, and the interpenetration between them.

Embarking on Therapy

Reasons for commencing therapy

What prompts the journey of therapy? In addition to symptoms of neurosis – anxiety, phobias, compulsions – the impetus may come from one or more of the following: addictions:

- Physical illness or disease

- Psychosomatic problems

- A life crisis

- Worries about sexual orientation

- Grief or any form of loss; loneliness; difficulty in relating to people

- Anger

- Guilt

- Disillusion, stagnation or depression

- A feeling that one's life lacks balance, is one-sided

- A sense of potential not yet fulfilled

- Regrets about past years wasted

- A realisation that one's personality lacks wholeness, perhaps because one is not listening to feelings, instincts or intuition – or to one's contra-sexual side

- Self-destructive tendencies and not learning from mistakes

- Loss of meaning and purpose

- A need to set new goals, and, by self-growth, to be able to approach these goals

In addition to these individual needs which prompt inner work, there is a universal, archetypal aspiration towards wholeness. One of the American astronauts, when he first set foot on the moon, said simply, 'I now realise there is a fundamental truth to our nature. People must explore.' We need exposure and risks. A desire to discover is in our genes. The Romans had a proverb about this basic human longing: *Tendimus in altum* ('We strive for the heights').

Two men – of different country, era and temperament – have written eloquently about the urgency for endeavour and work on oneself:

> If I shrink from the Call
> I lose my own soul.

> Henrik Ibsen, *Brand*

> On a huge hill,
> Cragged, and steep, Truth stands, and he that will
> Reach her, about must and about must go;
> And what the hill's suddenness resists, win so;
> Yet strive so, that before age, death's twilight,
> Thy soul rest, for none can work in that night,
> To will, implies delay, therefore now do.
> Hard deeds, the body's pains; hard knowledge too
> The mind's endeavours reach, and mysteries
> Are like the sun, dazzling, yet plain to all eyes.

> John Donne, 'Kind Pity Chokes My Spleen'

Goals

Now let us consider the subject of goals, as seen from a client's point of view. When starting therapy, the goals may be a combination of definite, articulated objectives ('I want to overcome this problem') and deeper, perhaps unspoken, ones ('I lack a sense of identity'). At first, a client may only feel an intuitive need for self-work; if so, time needs to be allowed for even initial goals to be articulated and crystallised.

In every session, at all stages of therapy, it is vital for the therapist to keep a joint view of both the immediate aims and the medium-term and long-term goals. In parallel with formulating and reformulating their hypothesis – the therapist will be watching for goal shifts.

Indeed, both therapist and client, guide and explorer, will need to watch for the way motives, expectations, needs and goals – overt and/or ultimate – may change while *en route*: partly because of inner unpeeling, layer by layer; partly because of new stimulus from outer events and encounters. In all types of journey, we to some extent decide the journey, but the journey also forms and shapes itself.

Contract

Just as a camp has a set of standing orders, so also therapy needs a form of contract, a clear understanding about certain issues – money, regularity of attendance, and openness (Freud's 'basic rule' about the client's non-censoring of thoughts, feelings or memories).

The reasons for various routines and disciplines will be explained by the therapist: in times of doubt or trouble, outer stability can help one through a period of inner and/or outer chaos. The rhythm is all.

These standing orders may be few in number, but adhering to them, or ignoring them, can mean the difference between survival and failure of the whole enterprise.

Agreement will be reached at least about the initial goal or goals, and about the main route. The guide may not have travelled personally across this particular area, but is confident about most types of terrain: jungle (confusion), desert (loneliness), mountains (major life events), river crossing (change).

Roles will be clarified, and expectations discussed. The guide will need to remind themselves and their companion (whom we shall call 'the explorer') about the difference between a guide and a leader. The aim is not for the explorer to become more like the guide, but more like their own self.

Fears when beginning or contemplating therapy

Journey is clouded with paradox. The very moment of high enthusiasm – the start – may also be, for an explorer or a client, a time of doubt and delay, sidestep or escape.

For a therapist, the first consultation requires the quality of attention of a surgeon: within an hour, they are absorbing dozens of facts, trying to formulate a hypothesis, dealing with some practical issues (such as the fee) and watching for early transference reactions.

At the start of most types of relationship, some communicating is in the form of coded messages. Thus, a potential client, when raising doubts about fees, distance to travel or appointment times, may also be expressing displaced anxiety. What, then, are the underlying fears?

1. Fear of a new view of the known. We are tempted to see some parts of our past as a golden age. But, on closer examination, buried hurts and forgotten mistakes may be unearthed.

2. Fear of letting go of old patterns. This fear may contain a deeper and ontological fear of being empty, once the false self has been unmasked.

3. Fear of losing direction and of getting totally lost. And a fear of severe, even a permanent, regression.

4. Fear of the unknown. And especially a fear of confronting (often from a basis of low self-esteem) one's shadow side; as well as a shyness about revealing it.

   Fear of the hidden may in time prove to have been worse than the reality. One of the most prized benefits of therapy is to overcome a fear of darkness. At some stages of a journey, such as in the desert, in order to avoid the heat of the daytime and to have stars as navigating points, it may be found to be easier to travel at night.

   > With their true life to make
   > In the depths of the dark,
   > If they could but endure;
   > Who flee from their dark star
   > Each from his own true self ...

   Ibsen, *Brand*

5. Fear that the goal may not be reached; or that the goal may prove to be illusory.

6. Fear of new challenges: unexpected in timing, type and size.

7. Fear of incapacity to meet challenges of a scale and complexity one has never before faced, knowing that things may get a lot worse before they get better. As Wittgenstein said, 'No wine without fermentation.'

A potential client may wonder if there is another easier or quicker type of journey or way of help and healing. Many of our cultural habits and influences offer quick, easy solutions: 'Take a pill,' or, 'Drown your sorrows.' How appealing to rely on an outside factor, or on someone else's authority and expertise, rather than commit oneself to a radical, pattern-jolting process – and a gradual one – which involves self-challenging, as well as work and re-forming self on the anvil of experience.

It takes faith and courage to hope that by exploring darkness you will emerge into the light. Monica Furlong wrote of 'the terrible cost of maturity' when newly facing your fears and desires, and your past.[35]

8. Fear that the therapist – whose strength and skills have yet to be tested and validated by the client – may not be able to share or shoulder the burdens, may not be able to go the full distance.

In a first consultation, the therapist may be able to offer a trial interpretation, linking this fear with the client's experience of grief and partings, and of unmet expectations – being let down.

9. And, lastly, that fundamental trilogy of deep doubts: resentment of dependence, reluctance to trust, and fear of disapproval, judgement and rejection.

Because of these fears – many in number and daunting in depth – it is no surprise that some potential therapeutic journeys never reach even the preparation stage.

One cannot overestimate what a formidable test this is for any therapist, no matter how experienced. The task here is to help the potential client to begin to articulate ambivalence: hope and fear, fascination as well as timidity, the call of

---

[35] Monica Furlong, *With Love to the Church* (London: Hodder and Stoughton, 1965).

aspiration and flinch of diffidence, engaging in secret struggle. And why? Because a summit is both alluring and alarming.

Jung saw mountain-climbing as one of man's archetypal goals, on which one projects both aspirations and anxieties. The Latin word *periculum* shows us this duality: it means 'attempt' and 'experiment', and also 'hazard', 'danger', 'peril'.

Ibsen, in several of his plays, reminds us that – in any aspect or field of life – the greater the potential gain, the greater the risk. Furthermore, gain and risk are intertwined. This poses a dilemma, a conflict, for a neurotic personality, because their main psychic aims are to play safe and to retain control. This makes them wary of any form of journey – travel or love or therapy – because journey entails the giving of oneself to a person, a partner, a process.

It is of the nature of most goals to be desirable but difficult to attain: difficult, but not impossible. And if people have already pioneered the route, this in no way diminishes – and by example may enhance – the value of successes in their own journeying.

Starting

To glimpse potential. To wish. A third thing is necessary: to dare.

However careful the preparation, much can only be verified *en route*: the developing of trust; finding a shared sense of pace; the constant need to adapt and improvise; learning about each other's limits.

The origin of the word 'journey' – from the word 'day' – reminds us of two things. The first is the need for regularity. However one is feeling, and whatever the weather – rain or sunshine or dullness – the two of them set out; the journey goes on.

Second, the cycle of the days enables them to make a new start: to forgive self and others; to resolve relationships, misunderstandings; to recover energy and morale; and to keep freshness of observation. Thus, regularity and newness are contrasting but complementary.

Therapeutic Stance and Process

Flexibility

For a therapist, it is wise to approach each session – and here I am speaking in relative terms – free of role and sense of status, without memory, and without expectation, to paraphrase Wilfred Bion.[36] The therapist is aware of the overall shape and possible span of the therapy; at the same time, he treats each day, each session, as a journey in itself.

No two journeys – even over the same territory – are the same. At every stage, constant flexibility, constant adapting to ever-changing conditions, will be needed, using various modes of transport and with differing speeds of progress.

Your place of focus varies also. Sometimes you have to look down at the ground and watch step by step; at other times you can look quite far into the distance without fear of losing your foothold.

The maturing of the psyche, and the gradual, lifelong discovering of one's essential self, is an organic process. As such, it is marked by stages. A pause can contribute to ultimate progress: you have time to reflect, and perhaps make or complete maps (of ground already covered). More strength of character may be needed to pause, to make a detour, to retrace your steps, or even to retreat, than to persist obstinately.

---

[36] See Wilfred Bion, 'Notes on Memory and Desire', *The Psycho-analytic Forum*, 1967, Vol. 2, No. 3.

You may encounter mist or fog and feel lost, and you may temporarily lose your bearings. One of my supervisors once said about his note-taking, 'After some sessions I write diagonally across a page of notes, "I don't know what is going on."' Only a man of stature could admit that – and especially to a group of trainees under his guidance.

If you are having difficulties in the inner life, or if outer circumstances are hostile, if a storm is approaching, or if you are in the middle of one, the thing to do is stay where you are, or go to nearby cover, keep dry and warm, conserve your energy and wait for the storm to subside. This is especially important if you are in an exposed position: on a boat, climbing a mountain, in a desert or working with the unconscious. St Ignatius' famous guideline – not to make any major change in a time of desolation – has been well tested and proved over time.[37]

Time

Whether standing still or on the move, the guide and the explorer will face questions of distance and time. At the very start, a therapist's technical skills are put to the test. If they speak realistically about the demands on time, on money and on emotional investment, the client may feel overawed.

But honesty and openness prompt the therapist to outline the potential long-term commitments. By giving a clear and firmly based framework, the therapist will also be giving reassurance that they are able and prepared to travel on the therapeutic journey for as long as proves necessary, and however hard the conditions. And by leaving the length of time open ended, they are indirectly affirming that the client and their own particular journey are unique.

---

[37] St Ignatius of Loyola; trans. Anthony Mottola, *The Spiritual Exercises of St Ignatius* (New York: Doubleday, 1989), pp. 82-87.

What is so fascinating is the way our perception of the passage of time is so subjective. We all notice this when we are walking. Excessive heat, ground that is rough or dull and unchanging in type of terrain, or the approach of dusk: all these can make a walk seem longer.

By contrast, a journey on which one is accompanied feels quicker, to the limbs and to the mind, than a solo journey. And the return usually seems rather faster than the outward half, even if both are over exactly the same route. In the longer perspective of time, some clients say that a two- or three-year period of therapy seems shorter when observed from the end of that period than when anticipated (warily) at the start.

Most crucially, the sense of time passing depends on two things: first, the rapport between therapist and client. This comes from being in step, and from a shared sense of pace. Sometimes these come naturally; sometimes they may need to be discussed. The second important element is momentum, which comes from several sources: awareness and observation; order and planning; aspiration; and the rhythm that comes from the rapport we have just mentioned. The journey then takes on its own momentum, as illustrated in a passage from Dante's *The Divine Comedy*:

> Now do I see that never can our intellect be sated, unless truth shine on it … And reach truth we must, else were all longing futile. Wherefore there springest a shoot of a plant, questioning, at the foot of truth; which is a thing that thrustest us towards the summit – ever onwards, from ridge to ridge.

Paradiso, canto 4

Landmarks

As we travel, we notice milestones or landmarks. These are symbols of progress, and they help us if we need to retrace our steps, either in the normal course of returning or because we took a wrong turn, or have confronted an obstacle and have to find another route.

A landmark may or may not have a name. And we may or may not know the name. But, to mark a stage of a journey, we choose a particular landmark – a river, a large rock, a tree – and we are free to give it our own choice of name.

I sometimes use this imagery in my work. When there is enough evidence to suggest that a client is on new ground, more solid ground, we may speak of reaching a new plateau. This suggests the setting-up of a base camp as a place for consolidation. And I may encourage the client to name the change and the plateau, in their own terms. One client, after about four years of therapy, said that, when walking in London, the city now seemed smaller and less intimidating.

A return journey, like the second half of a period of therapy, can help you to see and mark change. You may be covering similar ground, but you surmount obstacles with more ease. You move with a new sense of freedom, with more fluency, wider vision.

Naming

Let us take a further glance at the use and value of naming. A patient goes to the doctor's surgery and describes various symptoms. Eventually the GP names the condition. Uncertainty and the unknown were hard to bear. Some relief can come – even from hearing your doctor use a long Latin word!

In an early phase of therapy, many a client will ask, 'Are you familiar with my condition? Have you come across it before?'

To 'name' does not necessarily mean to 'label'. When talking with a client, the therapist may choose to avoid using jargon, but their recognition of a condition or group of symptoms is a form of naming. And equally important is the client's own description of feelings and symptoms, and their starting to dig down for roots and causes.

Naming externalises what may seem one-sidedly inside: for example, when a client is trying to reconcile opposite tendencies within self. Naming also helps them feel the commonality of a particular condition, and of suffering in general, after what may for a long time have seemed a singular – even an unknown-to-others – inner experience, mood or state. Thus naming can make something more bearable. Later, after some progress, naming helps a client inhabit and stay on new ground.

Changes resulting from therapy

What helps to bring about change?

A Catholic writer, Fr Raoul Plus, wrote about 'a creative descent to details'; and the Rev Dr P. T. Forsyth, a Scottish theologian, penned a marvellous and original phrase: 'the courage of the prosaic'.[38] Patient and careful attention to detail is earthing and reality giving. Because of the need to watch every step, a journey brings you more into the here and now. In the face of wind and rain, and the constant danger of slipping or falling, you need to be steady, vigilant. Danger or possible danger enforces alertness, body awareness and present awareness. Many clients, when they begin therapy, have limited present-moment focus: they are haunted by unresolved pain and issues of the past, and preoccupied with fears about the future.

---

[38] P. T. Forsyth (ed.), Jason A. Goroncy, *Descending on Humanity and Intervening in History: Notes from the Pulpit* (Oregon: Pickwick, 2013), p. 311.

As well as a new dwelling in present time, and a stronger adaptation to reality, therapy tends to yield changes to the client's ambitions, values, needs and pleasures. All the senses are heightened. The client is more accepting of their limitations. New-found parts of the self emerge. Past experiences are re-incorporated and become useful, available, in new and unexpected ways. Integration is forged between body and mind, intellect and feelings, inner life and the outer world. And they learn and embrace the rewards of risk.

From attention to small details, and from questions and issues shared with the therapist, a client gains a new way of seeing self, others, relationships and even their surroundings. They have new depth, alertness and continuity in their powers of observation. We have something of a parallel in bio-feedback. By becoming aware of brainwave patterns, blood pressure and heart palpitations, one's body may become self-correcting of imbalances.

The quality of perception and observation is one of the central gains of psychotherapy, and is the basic agent of transformation. By noticing the therapist's own self-awareness, by having hostile feelings accepted, and by being given time – and fullness of time, because of the therapist's attention – the client does much more self-listening, has more self-dialogue and self-trust, and gains in responsiveness and spontaneity. They are more 'in the moment'.

Only if we observe – accurately and acutely – do we have the chance to choose, to see and to seize opportunities, and to bring inner and/or outer change into our life.

To go on a journey is to learn more about one's capacities, limitations and previously hidden potential. It is to discover individuality and self-worth; to shake off the moulding and armouring and compromises of the collective norm, which have caused some loss of sense of self; and to shed the conditioning caused by the 'shoulds', 'oughts' and 'musts' of family life, school and the corporation.

Above all, relationships change. For example, much promiscuity is caused by fear: a fear that closeness will inevitably entail a further erosion of the sense of self. Hence the move to another relationship whenever a deeper level of intimacy is reached, which the person finds threatening. But, having grown through journeying, and with a new degree of self-possession, one re-enters relationships – and work, and one's links with the community – with less fear and more choice.

Dangers

At all stages, morale needs to be watched, and under-confidence or over-confidence guarded against. It is a paradox of journey that the time immediately before and after reaching the summit, the very moment of attainment, is dangerous and needs vigilance. The possible hazard is what Jungians call 'inflation'.

A further paradox, of both travel and a therapeutic journey, is that the descent can be more perilous than the ascent – because of outer, practical difficulties as well as because of a person's psychological state.

When you are seeking a goal, you need constantly to keep in mind that you are always near the edge, as you stretch beyond what you have hitherto regarded as your normal reach. To a degree, you have to be taken over by your goal and your searching for it. But being carried away by the goal can lead to being consumed by it. Unless you stay alert, unless you remain earthed, unless you have enough variety of interests in your life, then you may over-reach and become self-destructive and, in your downfall, hurtful to other people, especially those who are close to you. The art of goal-seeking, then, is to yield oneself to being carried along, but not carried away.

Failure?

Many more journeys are begun than completed, and this is for a variety of reasons, ranging from a fear of increasing dependence to a belief, possibly mistaken, that one has already learned all that the journey can teach.

If there is to be what feels to the therapist like a premature end, they should try to *make* the ending rather than let it happen in a ragged or haphazard way, as happens in so many other types of relationship: social, or commercial or professional.

If the debriefing is well handled, and if the client has felt able to give reasons and share open and honest reactions, they (the client) will feel more able to start again – should they wish to, at a later date – with the same therapist or with someone else. A good-enough ending makes possible a new beginning.

Failure may only be apparent. The client may have learned much: perhaps more than they or the therapist can at that time see. Gains may come months or years after a termination, and so both people need to take a long view of progress.

The only way for a therapist to achieve stability is to stand apart from, to transcend, notions of success and failure. If they briefly feel disheartened by what seems to have been a premature ending, they can remind themselves of two things: first, that whatever they have given – patience, acceptance, insight – will ultimately benefit the client. Second, and above all, they need to let go with dignity, and in a tone of calm self-worth.

Mutual learning

Two people who are roped together while climbing a mountain are mutually dependent, equally vulnerable, whatever their relative experience and ability, and whatever their relative status. In the consulting room, the balance of power is by no

149

means one-sided. For example, if the therapist is still in training, they may fear a premature termination by the client.

Equally, the learning need not be one-sided. If therapist and client both approach the work and their relationship in a spirit of learning, mutual learning, the client may point the way to territory new to both of them.

Winnicott dedicated one of his books to his patients, in gratitude for all that they had taught him. Freud declared that psychoanalysis began when one of his colleagues, Josef Breuer, treated Bertha Pappenheim (referred to as 'Anna O' in case-study material) with a therapeutic procedure which she herself helped to develop: she coined the term 'the talking cure'. Up to this time, Breuer had relied mainly on hypnosis.[39]

Freud's treatment of the 'Wolf-man' was groundbreaking in the early history and development of psychoanalysis. His work with another patient, Anna von Lieben (Freud called her his teacher), confirmed the value of the new talking cure.

Freud's method of free association was in part suggested to him by his patient, Elisabeth von R. In his description of his work with Elisabeth von R, we find Freud's first use of the term 'resistance', as well as his early formulations about defence mechanisms.[40]

One of the most original contributions of Jung, the other founding father of psychoanalysis, was to suggest that a main factor for change in a client is the therapist's continuing work on and in himself, as prompted by that client.

What a therapist can learn from their work is beyond price: for example, in more awareness of hidden anger, in the maturing of ambitions, in the increase of lucidity of expression, and in the growth of openness, insight and compassion. Each new stage of the therapist's life and work brings new areas of the self to be worked on.

---

[39] Sigmund Freud, *Five Lectures on Psycho-Analysis* (London: Penguin, 1995), pp. 8-9.
[40] Ernest Jones, *The Life and Works of Sigmund Freud* (London: Penguin 1964), p. 216.

Growing and healing, in both people, are more likely to come if the roles – of guide and explorer, therapist and client – are allowed to overlap to some extent. The model, then, is joint vulnerability and mutual learning.

Qualities and Attitude of the Therapist

Guide

What do we look for in a guide? Technical competence and compatibility. Someone who sets a tone – from the start – of joint decision-making. Someone who knows the pitfalls, who has been over the same or similar ground, and has been on testing journeys themselves. Above all, someone who is willing to be one step behind, allowing the other person to set the pace, and to choose when and where to stop for an exploration in depth.

One of the best guides in my life was my father. Only now do I fully appreciate how skilful he was, and also how subtle. My parents emigrated to Spain for their retirement, and a few years ago I went there to recuperate after an illness. I was then in my mid-thirties; my father was in his mid-sixties. What follows is based on extracts from a journal.

My father and I had an unspoken understanding that we would walk together every day, no matter what nature gave us: sun or storm. The initiative for our daily walk was left to me: he would indicate where he could be found, and when.

When we set out, he adjusted his step to mine, and asked, 'Which way, today?' We would discuss the possibilities, such as a stroll by the sea or, if we needed shelter, inland among pine trees, farms and orange groves. He left the final decision to me.

During the walk, using his knowledge of the locality, he might suggest variations to our basic route. This was partly to avoid boredom: he never liked to go twice on exactly the same circuit. Sometimes these variations were dictated by weather conditions, which on a small and exposed island could change quickly and dramatically.

My father was the first of us to climb over obstacles, such as stone walls or fences. Having done so, he showed me the best footholds and warned of any loose slats (in a fence) or loose stones. If I was slow in getting over a wall, or if I stumbled while walking or climbing, he never commented. He half-watched me, enough to guard my well-being, but he never watched over me to a degree that might have made me feel self-conscious. He was at all times a careful architect of space in our relationship.

Each of us was free to suggest a pause, either to rest or to observe our surroundings in detail: ships far out at sea, yachts in competition, spring flowers, or birds often of exotic colouring. During a pause, we might reflect on and discuss what we had seen so far.

Between our walks, I sometimes repeated a route on my own. The distance this second time usually seemed markedly shorter. I would often ask myself, 'What would Dad do here?' Perhaps my question has a parallel in what is termed 'the introjection of the analyst', namely the process whereby a patient or client, after the work has ended, has internalised the figure of the analyst and can image how he or she might respond.

A while later, I learned about several more aspects of my father's quiet and gentle guiding. He tried to shape each walk so that the second half – when my strength began to sag – was on easier terrain than the first part. Also, he learned to judge from my pace, early in each walk, how far I might be able to go on that day. And – unknown to me at the time – he very gradually increased the length of our walks in proportion to my recovery.

One of the most vital and valuable elements of good journeying, and of good-enough therapeutic work, is care about pacing. Correct pacing enhances a therapist's sense of timing, such as when to offer an interpretation, and correct pacing gives a client the basic and longed-for reassurance that they are being seen in their own personhood and individuality: 'He adjusted his step to mine.'

In addition to his sense of pace, my father was adept at listening below the surface, such as for buried fears or hopes. And the very essence of skilled work with people is to attend to their choice of words and tone of voice; to observe the subtle and hidden; the unspoken; a gap in a narrative; the hesitation; the half-gesture, a shift of posture; a brief, seemingly casual, throwaway remark; discord between words and affect, and discord between content of material and body language; and the as-yet-unasked question – the content of the unconscious which is about to come to the surface. In short, to give one's whole attention to the whole person.

One of Thomas Merton's friends said, 'When we talked, I told him a few things; and he understood the things I didn't tell him. He was open to everything.'[41]

We have in our language an evocative expression: 'to find one's feet'. The French versions of this are equally vivid, and are apt in relation to our subject of journey. There are three main ones. In translation, they mean, 'to begin to feel one's feet', 'to become disentangled', and 'to fly by one's own wings'. Psychotherapy offers a variant: to grow in therapy comes from being given the space – an accepting, self-defining atmosphere – in which to find and to use one's own true voice.

In those journal notes about my father, I see many of the ingredients of good therapeutic practice: his leaving the initiative to me; his knowledge of the ground; his benign neutrality; his watchfulness; the confidence I had in him, and the confidence he gave me in myself; and, above all, his modesty and self-effacement. This last quality is a subject we shall return to for a closer look.

---

[41] Quoted in Matthew Fox, *Thomas Merton's Creation Spirituality Journey* (New World Library, 2016), p. 23.

Qualities

Many are the qualities needed to be a guide: imagination and the ability to plan, as well as practical skills; flexibility, quick-wittedness and the ability to improvise; relish of a challenge; faith, single-mindedness and conviction; self-discipline; self-reliance, as well as a capacity for cooperation; mental stamina; willpower; courage.

There is one further basic quality, and it would feature high on my own list of aspirations: perseverance. A willingness to continue even when the conditions and the odds seem to be against you. An aide said to Odysseus, 'You are one of those hard men, whose spirit never flags, and whose body never tires. You must be made of iron.'

Most of these qualities are needed in some degree; each guide will have them in different proportions. And by the osmosis of the therapeutic journey, a client may develop some of these strengths.

All these are qualities needed for survival. What is so interesting is the number of similarities between two lists: one such as would be compiled by a therapist for his profession; and the other for a mountaineer or a commando.

Hesitancy

When I mentioned to a colleague the title for this chapter, he said with a smile, 'I'm all for hesitancy.' This is a brave and original thing to say in an age when the watchwords are, 'can do', 'hands on', 'proactive', 'tackle things head-on', and, 'go for it'.

To hesitate means to be unsure – but not necessarily in the sense of dithering. To be unsure can be uncomfortable, but may also be creative: making us watchful, alert, resourceful.

In its Latin origin, to hesitate means 'to hold back in doubt' or 'to be (temporarily) fixed in one position'. At some stages of a journey, this is the appropriate state to be in. As President Eisenhower said, with an Oscar Wildean inversion, 'Don't just do something. Stand there.'

For a therapist, to be hesitant can be a safeguard against the trap that lurks around every corner: over-activity (during a session). In 1991, Dr William Piper of the University of Alberta analysed 22,500 therapist interventions from audio tapes of sessions. He found that the more interpretations a therapist made, the worse the outcome for the patient.[42]

Just as love is best given discreetly, so also the ways of the therapist are subtle. Much of their work is hidden; and the results, if any, are often obscure and/or delayed. They have to expect to do much of their work in the dark. They have to be prepared to be let down, sometimes to feel uncertain of the direction of things, and often to be unthanked.

If the therapist has a faith, they will be helped by grace to find new reserves of stamina; and the capacity to keep on making allowances for the client's behaviour, while not letting themselves be manipulated.

Results

A spirit or state of humility helps a therapist to be non-possessive. They will keep in mind the help and support given to a client before therapy began. And the therapist will be willing to be assisted, indirectly, by others (such as the client's GP practice), and not try to become the sole source of sustaining activity.

Humility also helps a therapist work towards being non-attached to results. Change is to be allowed to come – if at all – in its own way, and in its own time.

[42] William E. Piper, Anthony S. Joyce, Mary McCallum and Hassan F. A. Azim, 'Concentration and Correspondence of Transference Interpretations in Short-Term Psychotherapy', *Journal of Consulting and Clinical Psychology* 113, Vol. 61. No 4, pp. 586-595.

It is far more important that one's life should be
perceived than that it should be transformed; for
no sooner has it been perceived, than it
transforms itself of its own accord.[43]

Jung believed in the innate, self-regulating capacity of both
the body and the psyche, to seek self-healing and wholeness,
through the reconciliation of one's opposite tendencies.

Why should a therapist expect to *see* results? If they are a
believer, they will regard themselves as a co-worker in and for
God's kingdom: we live and we die in the middle of that
continuous drama of salvation which is this life here on earth.
The death of Christ on the cross marked a beginning, as well as
a completion. The failure of Good Friday was only an apparent
failure, and the tears of Calvary gave way to the joy and
triumph of the Resurrection.

---

[43] Maurice Maeterlinck, trans. Alfred Sutro, 'The Deeper Life' in *The Treasure
of the Humble* (London: George Allen, 1897), p. 185.

Pain and Growth

Pain and growth are linked. We find this, for example, when a baby is cutting new teeth, when a teenager has 'growing pains', and when a woman is giving birth. What is true of the body is also true for the psyche. We grow by surviving pain. And we grow by testing ourselves against events or challenges. To test oneself to the limit is one way of learning about oneself: joggers and marathon runners learn what it is to go past the 'pain barrier'.

It has been said: no endurance, no triumph. In order to grow, in order to achieve inward elevation, we may actually need a period of privation or struggle. This is part of our human blueprint: until we have struggled, we do not really know our self. Odysseus realised this: 'My strength has been developed and proved in suffering.'

In some so-called primitive cultures, initiation rites use pain as a way to symbolise entry to adult society and adult identity. Let any society beware if it does not offer – and keep devising – *appropriate* initiation rites. Today, many teenage cultures, and increasingly some pre-teenagers (because of the earlier onset of puberty and stronger influences from adolescents), are concocting their own rites. Listen to the brutality behind these words, which on the surface have a catchy, sing-song quality: street cred, lager lout, quick lay, gang bang, needle fix, rent boy, ramraiding (driving a stolen car into a shop). These are worldwide trends of self-destruction and damage to other people and their property. All this energy, and this need for a rite of passage, needs to be rechannelled into positive directions.

We have yet to discover effective and widely usable ways of counteracting the life-lowering effects of overcrowding and passive use of leisure time. Social change and technological change seem to be fast outpacing our finding of new and worthwhile personal challenges. As seen from the time-perspective of evolution, we have moved rapidly from the hunter-gatherer of tribal society to the starer-at-a-screen of the age of high technology.

We live in a second-hand society. Many people have a tendency to watch rather than participate. Most of us pluck fruit, plastic wrapped, from a supermarket shelf rather than from a tree. Surrogate motherhood makes even childbirth second-hand. But the essence of journey – inner or outer – is that the experience is first-hand.

The human skills, qualities and instinctual drives that were once needed for survival have to be kept useful and creative by our finding new goals. As scope for new discovery of the earth diminishes, and while the costs of space exploration remain daunting, it is natural that we should quest inwardly. To be fully alive means to retain a spirit of adventure.

Oneness

A major paradox is that growth, in selfhood and independence, is combined with a realisation of healthy dependence: on weather, the environment, a guide, fellow travellers. We are reminded simultaneously of the littleness and of the greatness of humanity.

Increased understanding and acceptance of self leads to more understanding and acceptance of other people. Working on one's own needs helps one to feel less apart, because of learning simultaneously more about the struggles and suffering of other people. One's life gains a new and wider context.

From the summit, we can see that struggles or travels cover shared ground. From the isolation of a valley to partnership on our journey to oneness at the mountain top – then able to look freely in all directions. People may have used different routes to come to the top of a mountain. From there, but only from there, everyone can share the same view.

We may then come to see that people on other types of endeavour – religion, the arts, ecology – share what Tillich called 'ultimate concern'; and that these people and their journeys all have the same ultimate destination, just as different radii of a circle point to a shared centre.

Keats, when he was 22, wrote:

> But the Minds of Mortals are so different and bent on such diverse journeys that it may at first appear impossible for any common taste and fellowship to exist ... It is however quite the contrary. Minds ... leave each other in contrary directions, traverse each other in numberless points, and at last greet each other at the journey's end.

> Letter to John Hamilton Reynolds, 19 ii 1818

There is a fundamental link between the one and the many. The more you are experiencing in your own journey, and the more you are learning from this (such as reconciling some of your opposites), the more you gain in security of self-identify. You come to your own true individuality and personhood. From this new vantage point, being more integrated and at one, you can reach out to the many, and accept and appreciate the different journeys of other people.

Destination

In religious terms, the destination is God: to see Him in all things, in all people, in every experience. This is the finding of ultimate meaning, and gives unity and continuity to the whole life journey.

In psychological terms, the destination is the discovery and balanced use of the true self: a re-owning, a re-inhabiting, of the self. The psychological journey will aid the spiritual quest but will not take one into the heights (or depths) to which prayer leads.

> The longest journey
> Is the journey inwards,
> Of him who has chosen his destiny,
> Who has started upon his quest
> For the source of his being...

> Dag Hammarskjöld, *Markings*[44]

The end of a period of therapy is a new beginning. The traveller (of a few months or years) becomes a long-term, lifelong explorer. We may then ask: When does Journey in the deepest sense begin? And when – if ever – does it end?

> So deep is the soul, you would not find the boundaries of the soul, even by travelling along every path.

> Heraclitus, On Nature, *The Cosmic Fragments*[45]

---

[44] Trans. W. H. Auden and Leif Sjöberg, *Markings* (London: Faber and Faber, 1964), p. 65.
[45] Trans. G. S. Clark, *The Cosmic Fragments* (Cambridge: Cambridge University Press, 1954).

THE SECRET

Privacy

It does seem to be a paradox to be writing about the archetype of the Secret. I am reminded of Yehudi Menuhin, who once gave a talk about silence. Three opening questions occur to me in this regard: What is happening to our concept of time? What is happening to the concept of privacy? Are these changes related?

Consider these much-used expressions of recent years: 'quick fix', 'sound bite', 'short-termism', the 'credit card society', the 'Now generation', 'split-second timing'. Advertisements offer instant loans and fast relief from pain.

The world is in a manic phase. We talk faster, we move faster, and workers sweat and strain to keep up with clank and shudder of the assembly line. Population growth creates competitiveness, fear, war, a fight for survival and for diminishing natural resources. Our concept and experience of time has become tense, impatient and one-sided.

An over-focus on the NOW is also to be seen in the whole area of self-expression, and self-expression is closely related to Secret; we are encouraged to act on impulse. This can result in a one-night stand, in which the secret of self and the secret of sex are too suddenly exposed.

We are also encouraged to reveal the secrets of our past and present, but the virtue of being open is infected by the vice of invasion of privacy. The chastity of reticence is being seduced by an attitude of premature and non-selective disclosure – of one's body, one's mind and one's memory.

If a secret is given away too soon or superficially, the inner self is robbed, and the inner self is close to what we mean by 'soul'. Suffering such a loss, a person seeks compensation – often in the form of craving: drugs, alcohol, violence, promiscuity. Because compensation is looked for outside, the craving is never satisfied.

If, by contrast, we guard our inner truth, we are selective about what we say. We reveal our deeper self only within a close relationship, and we do so gradually, spontaneously, at appropriate moments.

The Dutch theologian Henri Nouwen reminds us that:

> real openness to each other also means a real closedness, because only he who can hold a secret can safely share his knowledge … Just as words lose their power when they are not born out of silence, so openness loses its meaning when there is no ability to be closed.[46]

The phrase 'invasion of privacy' is accurate psychologically: not only the body but also the mind, the memory and the psyche can be raped. What do we feel are the natural boundaries for a public interview these days when, to mention just one recent example, a woman is asked in about half an hour about her dreams, her lack of children, her frequency of depression, her thoughts about death and her experience of brutal sex?

How wise are those tribal people who shy away from a camera. To go public about one's essence is to lose some of that essence. What will the results, the retribution, be from this invasion of privacy? A taboo trampled on will exact revenge.

To return to our opening questions: time and Secret are, indeed, related. The Latin word *prudens* means 'prudent'; it also means 'far-seeing'. Thus to be prudent entails a cautious view of time; the need to watch and wait. As a society, we need to restore the balance between the joys of having and the joys of

---

[46] Henri Nouwen, *Reaching Out: The Three Movements of the Spiritual Life* (New York: Doubleday, 2000).

waiting. Too much too soon – perhaps this is a main cause of that existential emptiness which so many young people feel.

The professional secret

Even a few analysts are weakening the boundaries between public and private. In a recent biography of a famous musician who died a few years ago, her psychoanalyst was quoted. He gave some intimate details of what had been confided to him. He justified these public disclosures on the grounds that his former patient had herself told various people about her own analysis.

By contrast, consider the noble example of Jung. In 1959, during a television interview in the BBC *Face to Face* series, there was this exchange:

> John Freeman: Tell me, did Freud himself ever analyse you?
>
> Jung: Oh yes, I submitted quite a lot of my dreams to him, and so did he.
>
> John Freeman: And he to you?
>
> Jung: Yes, oh yes.
>
> John Freeman: Do you remember now at this distance of time what were the significant features of Freud's dreams that you noted at the time?
>
> Jung: Well that is rather indiscreet to ask. You know I have ... There is such a thing as a professional secret.
>
> John Freeman: He's been dead these many years.
>
> Jung: Yes, but these regards last longer than life. (Pause) I prefer not to talk about it.

What a model for us all in our therapeutic work: integrity in both senses of that word – the integrity of oneness, wholeness; and the integrity of ethical truth. A lesser man – especially after

a major split such as occurred between Freud and Jung –
would have seized this chance and used it for revenge and
point-scoring. No, our duty of confidentiality extends beyond
the grave. Whether our listening role occurs in the context of
therapy or of ministry or pastoral care, we can help to rescue
and preserve the archetype of Secret.

The client's responsibility

What part does the client have in maintaining the therapeutic
container? Here is a helpful parable from *The Discourses* (Book
IV, chapter VIII), of Epictetus, a man who offers a supreme
example of individuation: a former slave who became one of
the great Stoic philosophers:

> Practise first not to let men know who you are;
> keep your philosophy to yourself a little while.
> That is the way the fruit is produced: the seed has
> to be buried and hidden for a season, and be
> grown by slow degrees, in order that it may come
> to perfection. But if it heads out before it
> produces the jointed stock, it never matures.[47]

In my own practice, I encourage clients to say little or
nothing about our work. I have developed this not because of
training (surprisingly, this aspect was seldom mentioned) but
because of belief and experience that all inner journeys –
whether of artistic creation or psychotherapy or the search for
God – need privacy.

In our work, transference is a major agent for change, and
transference should not be leaked outside. A client told me a
few weeks ago about a friend of his who is thinking of starting
therapy. This friend had said, 'But if I go into therapy I would

---

[47] Epictetus, trans. Robert Dobbin, *Discourses and Selected Writings* (London:
Penguin, 2008), Book IV, Chapter VIII.

have to tell my parents.' If a therapist were to question 'have to', this would bring two benefits: it would help the therapy by guarding the transference, and it would assist the client's creative separation from his parents – by making the very fact of being therapy, as well as what happens in therapy, a private matter.

Reluctance to Share

The content of the secret will vary according to the client's personality type, personal history and family taboos, as well as collective taboos. Collective taboos vary according to era and culture (national culture as well as racial culture).

The magnitude of the secret will vary according to the client's own and unique perception. What may at first seem to be a small secret to the therapist may loom large for the client, and what may seem large to the therapist may feel small to the client. Here, of all times, a client-centred approach is vital.

A client may hesitate to disclose a secret for several reasons, such as shame, or secondary gain, in which neurotic safety is preferred to risky change. Another reason for hesitation is to be found in the link between the secret and the transference. During childhood and teenage years, the capacity to keep one's secrets is a vital part of forming identity. In the transference (because therapy is a form of new growth, even sometimes rebirth, and because the therapist may be seen as a parent figure), the client may hold on to the Secret. But in the early stages of therapy we cannot assume that the client knows much about their secret: it may be lurking in his unconscious or pre-conscious. He may have a sense of inner ground to be explored: this hunch will carry hope and, maybe, even urgency, but also a threat of the unknown. Thus a useful point of technique is to help the client to voice feelings of ambivalence about the therapy, even if the cause of those feelings is for the time being still hidden, so that the ambivalence does not harden into outright resistance and/or premature negative transference.

Receiving the Other's Secret

How do we relate to a client's secret not yet disclosed, but which our intuition can sense? Here is where therapy becomes an art. There are further questions: How can we convey an atmosphere of sincerity, fostering trust? For how long do we collude with denial (in the clinical sense of that word)? How far do we, perhaps in indirect and allusive ways, assist a client in speaking of the repressed? Also, after a secret has been revealed, do we gently encourage elaboration of this secret and, perhaps, a revealing of others? And how long do we collude with a client's notion that their basic trauma or secret is the cause and source of all their problems?

There can be no clear formulae, but there are guidelines. We continue to be watchful and to rely on our instincts. We respect, as well as work with, the client's ambivalence. We quieten our own fascination with the Secret. We help to give substance to the secret and its causes and effects, but we do not get over involved; and we are careful not to be beguiled by fiction, fantasy or exaggeration. I shall return to this later (see 'Not colluding with distortions').

We notice the timing of the revealing of the secret in relation to the overall span of the therapy: for example, a premature disclosure might make the client retreat temporarily, fearing they have given away too much.

We observe the effect of the revealed secret on the therapy and the transference. How does the client see you, consciously and unconsciously, now that you are a sharer (perhaps the only one) of their secret? They have endowed you with new power in the relationship, and this potential power may be feared.

171

Also, the client may have a new sense of power and control, and may try to manipulate through what they share or do not share with you.

By contrast, a client who tends to be compliant may now fear that, because they have run out of 'big' material, he is not meeting the expectations of the therapist.

The revealed Secret brings many changes to the work: some are subtle, some overt, some of seismic proportion. At this stage, we need to be alert, offering interpretations carefully timed and carefully weighted – or, we could say, carefully waited and carefully weighted!

Above all, we continuously monitor variations in our stance or distance. Many, perhaps most, of our clients have suffered in childhood from extremes of closeness and aloofness. Based on a family in which both the parents are in the home, there are several variations: one parent too close, the other at a moderate distance; one parent aloof; both parents too close; both aloof; one or both aloof but invasive; one aloof and one too close; or, just as troublesome and sometimes more damaging than these fixed positions, having one or both parents who were moody and who would switch, sometimes suddenly, from love to seeming rejection. Sometimes there are links between a client's psychopathology and the specific form of parental configuration they experienced.

I promised at the beginning to suggest why the archetype of Secret is fundamental to our work. We have just now been looking at the heart of the matter: the centrality of Secret in therapy is because the way we handle the Secret (our moment-by-moment seeking for the right stance) gives the client what may be a once-in-a-lifetime opportunity to repair distortions that have lived on into adulthood.

The distasteful secret

A severe test for every therapist, no matter how experienced, is, 'What do we do, or refrain from doing, when confronted by a distasteful secret, such as sexual perversions or any form or degree of violence?' It is a daunting situation, but one which can be addressed in a number of ways:

First, see the client as a victim, someone with an unconscious compulsion to repeat or mirror past experiences to hurt others as they were once hurt.

Second, search for the root and cause of the present behaviour.

Third, feel free, within a framework of neutrality, to be natural, human and spontaneous, perhaps by showing non-judging awe in body language at what has been shared.

Fourth, pick up transference reactions, such as by asking the client how they expected their secret to be received.

Fifth, consider using a combination of cognitive therapy and transactional analysis, in which you encourage more dialogue between the client's inner voices. For example, their inner parent or inner adult could speak to the child, the part that impulsively clamours, 'I want, I must have.'

Sixth, work with counter-transference reactions, such as this new challenge to one's self-image of being non-judgemental.

Trust the client's psyche

With good reason, psychoanalysis has been called 'the impossible profession'. Sometimes, and especially when we are working with the Secret, we feel we are walking gingerly on a tightrope; but, accepting our flaws and our gifts, we can often recover from mistakes or mis-steps, such as temporary over-involvement.

At the very end of a recent session, a client – who has been coming for about a year – said he was afraid of being judged. He had just told me about some investments and was concerned that I, like his parents, might see him as being materialistic. We looked at the transference implications. He then said, 'I can now see that there are other private things I have not yet told you for fear of being judged.' I found myself encouraging him to trust his psyche: to reveal what it wants to reveal and when it wants to reveal.

I simultaneously said to myself that my role is to set an atmosphere – open, unjudging and alert – in which his psyche, having produced purposeful symptoms, can now do its own self-healing. The psyche, like all creation, has an urge to be free.

I find this a liberating model. The psyche, or soul, is an entity that is alive and intelligent. The client's psyche controls the pace of therapy, the timing and the content of the material. My role, our role, is to be a partner, a co-watcher, at the gate, the growing edge of the client's psyche.

Not colluding with distortions

Earlier, I said I would suggest ways of avoiding the lure of a client's fantasy or sustained exaggerations. There are four things we can do to encourage truth and accuracy in a client's presentation of their material:

First, by giving the client the assurance of total confidentiality: the secret truth must not be betrayed.

Second, by our reflecting material back to the client. They may thus, in a neutral and non-judging way, be helped to hear their own distortions.

Third, by our being well centred. If you are listening from your centre, you will encourage the other person to speak from their centre.

Fourth, something subtle and central: what is our stance to the whole person, and how much space are we giving to their material, and to their psyche? Can we be involved and yet non-possessive? Non-possessive involvement is warm and whole-hearted, and at the same time calm and detached.

We live in an era which presumes that more and more details will give a clearer and deeper view of the person, hence the probing tone of many media interviews and the photographing of celebrities. But the glory and salvation of a human being is that their being, their personhood, eludes capture. Their essence remains essentially secret.

Everything depends on the atmosphere we convey as we enter the consulting room. We are knowing but unknowing (unknowing in the sense of being free of expectation). Ideally, we combine the experience and wisdom of our years with a pure and innocent eye. To quote Monet, 'Whatever the cost or sacrifice, preserve the child's eye.'

BEETHOVEN: MAN OF COURAGE

Nathan Milstein

When I kneel in front of the gates of heaven, seeking to be let in, I expect to be examined on four subjects: love, family life and friends; integrity and moral behaviour; work; and leisure interests.

When St Peter asks about my leisure interests, this is what I plan to say:

> One especially good memory, Your Grace. And one failure. And they both involved the same person – the violinist Nathan Milstein. The joy was that I shook hands with him after a concert outside the artists' entrance at the Festival Hall. The failure was that I had an open invitation to go to his home, but I never did.

A friend of mine, Elisabeth, an American violinist, studied with Milstein. She had read my book of conversations with Yehudi Menuhin and she knew I might be interested in doing a similar book with Nathan Milstein. With his permission, she gave me his ex-directory phone number. I did ring it once, and spoke to his wife, but he was abroad on a long concert tour. I confess, with a blush of shame, that I didn't try to phone again.

Perhaps it is not always wise to meet our heroes or heroines: in face-to-face contact, they may not live up to our lofty expectations.

However, when I got to know Yehudi Menuhin, he turned out to be an even kinder and more welcoming person than I could have imagined, or hoped for. So why did I hesitate about meeting Nathan Milstein – especially given that we could have produced a book together? To this day it remains one of the major question marks of my life.

As a young boy, Milstein was a tearaway. A well-meaning (and prescient) neighbour told his mother, 'You must keep Nathan busy. Find him a music teacher.' Of such spontaneous advice, history is sometimes made.

He studied with Pyotr Stolyarsky in Odessa, and then at the St Petersburg Conservatory under the eminent Hungarian Leopold Auer, himself a soloist of repute, and one of the finest teachers of violin of that (or any other) era. Auer's other pupils included Heifetz, Elman and Zimbalist. Some progeny!

Milstein made his début in 1915, at the age of ten, in a concert to mark the fiftieth birthday of Glazunov. Milstein played the Glazunov Violin Concerto, with the composer conducting.

In 1921 Milstein teamed up with his legendary compatriot, the pianist Vladimir Horowitz. They toured the world, winning acclaim from critics and audiences. Later, they formed a trio when they were joined by an equally famous Russian musician, the cellist Gregor Piatigorsky.

If pushed into a corner and asked for my list of the top half-dozen violinists of the twentieth century, Milstein would be joined by (in no specific order) Ysaÿe, Heifetz, Kreisler, Menuhin and Elman.

Compared with most of the young virtuosi of our day, Milstein set a careful limit to his yearly number of concerts and recitals. By conserving his energy and his artistic libido, Nathan Milstein built a career with his violin which – for length (more than 60 years), consistent quality of musicianship and immaculate technique – has (if perhaps equalled) never been surpassed in the history of music.

Later, I shall outline some of the special features of his playing. At this stage, I'd like to tell you about his appearance, his platform manner.

Milstein was just below medium height. He used to bound up the stairs to the platform in a brisk, business-like way. During the opening *tutti*, he would gently sway, attuning himself to the majesty of the music and getting ready for the challenge to come. Sometimes he added gold to the orchestral tone by playing along with the first violins for a few bars. In repose, his face was a picture of relaxed concentration, the eyes closed or half-veiled. It was as though his playing was a form of meditation.

A few bars before the end of the work, I could sense a pent-up excitement among the whole audience. They (or, more correctly, *we*) usually gave him a standing ovation. During prolonged applause, Milstein was characteristically humble. The way he held his bow and violin in front of him, as he bowed to the audience, seemed to say, 'Please cheer my lovely Strad as well.'[48]

His order of priority was: first, the composer; second, the music; third, his violin; fourth, the audience; fifth and last, the projection – through music – of himself.

Here is a paradox: Milstein's technique inspires awe (even from the most gifted of fellow violinists), but his facility does not call attention to itself. In sensitive hands, technique is transcended, as the servant of high art. Milstein was a modest maestro: therein is the secret of his nobility. I salute his memory.

---

[48] Milstein's favourite instrument was a 1716 Stradivarius. He seldom taught, and when he did the arrangement was informal and unpaid.

Beethoven: Man of Courage

Origins

Of the seven children born to Johann and Maria van Beethoven, only three survived infancy. Ludwig (the second-born) was three and a quarter when (Caspar Anton) Carol was born, and almost six when (Nikolaus) Johann was born. Relations between Ludwig and his brothers were, at best, uneasy; at worst (which was often), they were combative – with fists as well as angry words.

It is sobering to reflect that, had Beethoven been conceived in our day, and given the medical history of both wings of his family, the embryonic Ludwig would have been a prime candidate for an abortion.

Mother

Just after her sixteenth birthday, Maria Magdalena married a valet, Johann Laym. They had a son who died in infancy. Just under three years after the marriage, her husband died. Not yet 19, she was already a widow and had lost a baby son. In a little less than two years, she remarried – this time to another Johann: Johann van Beethoven.

Just over a year after her second marriage, Maria's mother died; she had already mourned the early loss of her father. To recap, she had lost (in this order) father, first child, first husband, and then her mother. She was only 22. For these reasons (and others which I shall relate), it is not surprising that a neighbour (Cäcilia Fischer) could not recall that she had ever seen Frau van Beethoven laugh.

Maria also had to cope with (as we shall see later) a weak-willed husband, limited housekeeping money, her own fragile health, and the frustration of not being able to pacify the ongoing tension among her three boys, nor quell Johann's alcohol excesses. She died of tuberculosis, aged 40, when Ludwig was 16. Throughout his life he spoke of her in warm but non-specific terms: 'my excellent (*vortreffliche*) mother'.

Given her domestic burdens, frequent pregnancies and the many early losses of loved ones, we may wonder how much time or energy Maria had to nurture the emotional life and general development of her eldest son. Moreover, we have no evidence to suggest that any adult of the extended family was close to Ludwig, served as a role model or played a major part in his upbringing.

Beethoven and women

Beethoven dallied with many women. He never married. Although he told (and wrote to) close male friends about his desire for a lifelong companion, he may have deemed himself unfit for domestic life (as, for different reasons, his father had been). In Ludwig's case, there was the high hurdle of temperament, and the even higher barrier of his all-compelling profession. In the dedication of Three Piano Sonatas (WoO 47, 1783) to the Elector of Cologne, the 12-year-old wrote, 'Music became my first youthful pursuit in my fourth year.' But we may well ask, 'Did Beethoven, as boy or man, have any other significant pursuit?'

It may be no coincidence that Beethoven so often fell in love with unattainable women: young pupils, married women and (in a class-conscious age) members of the aristocracy. The fact is that music (indeed, any form of creativity) is a jealous mistress.

Live only in your Art!

Notebooks, 1816

Father

The composer's paternal grandfather (also named Ludwig, but known as Louis) had a fine bass voice, and (given that he seems not to have been a composer) was fortunate to be appointed *Kapellmeister*, with responsibility for supervising the music at the Bonn court.

Johann (the composer's father) was the third-born and only surviving child. His mother Josepha (the composer's maternal grandmother) became addicted to strong drink: it is possible that an underlying predisposition was heightened by the loss of two children. In his later years, her husband worked in the wine trade.

Like his father, Johann entered the Elector's service – first as a boy soprano; then, after adolescence, as a tenor in the chapel. He boosted his income by giving lessons in singing and clavier-playing to children of prominent Bonn families.

Ludwig's first teacher (of piano and violin) was his father, who seems to have inherited his mother's volatile temper. Beethoven's chief biographer, Thayer (an American with a zest for interview and research), writes of 'the inflexible severity with which the boy was kept at his musical studies'.[49] We have at least three first-hand accounts of people who recalled seeing the tiny boy in tears as he stood on a footstool in front of the clavier.

What was fuelling Johann's ambitions for his son? In 1763 (when Johann was in his early twenties), Mozart and his sister, Nannerl, had visited Bonn (Ludwig's birthplace). Johann wanted his eldest son to emulate Mozart, and tour the music

---

[49] Alexander Wheelock Thayer, *The Life of Ludwig Van Beethoven* (New York: General Books, 2009).

centres of Europe. But the more Johann pushed or bullied, the more the already strong-willed Ludwig resisted. No one, least of all his father, was going to market him as Mozart Mark II.

Ludwig soon needed more advanced instruction in music than his father could provide. From around 1782 he enjoyed the altogether more benign influence of Christian Gottlob Neefe, an organist and musical director of a theatre company. The young Beethoven may also have benefited from Neefe's interest in literature.

Johann began to drink heavily (as his mother had done) before his wife died in July 1787. Having for years left most of the parenting to his wife, he was not about to become a self-sacrificing single parent. On one occasion, Ludwig saved his intoxicated father from being arrested by the police.

In 1789 (when he was still only 18), Ludwig won a petition (made to the Elector) for half of his father's income so that he and his two younger brothers could be an independent family unit, headed by Ludwig. In addition, his father was put under threat (should he be guilty of any major misbehaviour) of being banished from Bonn.

The Elector dispensed with Johann's services as a court musician. (He might have dismissed him in any case because his voice had been deteriorating – mainly, no doubt, because of his drinking bouts.) For the welfare of all three boys (and specifically for the education of the two younger brothers), and out of special regard for Ludwig, the Elector kept Johann on a retainer – albeit entailing a reduction in annual income. Three years later (December 1792), Johann died. Ludwig's act of Oedipal conquest has intrigued biographers ever since.

Rebel

Partly because of the wary, resistant relationship he had with his father, Beethoven never deferred to authority or to the aristocracy. He saw it as no part of his nature or destiny to play the part of fawning courtier, forever flattering his master.

I hardly yet have learn'd
To insinuate, flatter, bow, and bend my knee.

Shakespeare, *Richard II*, IV i

Haydn, Salieri, and Johann Georg Albrechtsberger – three composers who taught Beethoven – all thought highly of him as a musician; but they were also united in their opinion of him as a pupil. They all said that Beethoven was so unyielding, so determined to get his own way, that he had to learn many things through painful experience (trial and error) which earlier he had refused to accept from instruction.

Give sorrow leave a while to tutor me
To this submission.

Shakespeare, *Richard II*, IV i

Beethoven's often-suspicious nature led to many arguments and misunderstandings – even with close friends. But he was usually prompt (in person and/or by letter) to express regret and seek reconciliation.

Education

After the age of 11, Beethoven had no regular schooling: this allowed him to concentrate all his time and faculties on music. In Bonn at that time, few children (even from wealthy families) went on from elementary school to a Gymnasium (high school).

Beethoven never mastered even simple arithmetic, and his punctuation was at best occasional. In his later years, his handwriting was usually no better than a scrawl.

Beethoven's formal education was short and not of the first quality, but – being a man of great vitality and questing intellect – he was, throughout his life, ever eager to study and explore.

He knew Latin, Italian and French: indeed, he sometimes wrote letters in French. He was learned in philosophy – Persian, Egyptian and Hindu.

His library included Kant's *Theory of the Heavens*, the plays of Shakespeare, Plutarch's *Lives*, much of Cicero, the complete works of Goethe and Schiller, *The Imitation of Christ*, and the Bible in German, French and Latin.

Method of composing

Louis Schlösser, a violinist in the Darmstadt court orchestra, asked Beethoven how he composed. Here is the illuminating reply:

> I carry my thoughts about with me for a long time, sometimes a very long time, before I set them down. At the same time, my memory is so faithful to me that I am sure not to forget a theme – which I have once conceived – even after years have passed.
>
> I make many changes, reject and reattempt, until I am satisfied. Then the working-out – in breadth, length, height and depth – begins in my head; and, since I am conscious of what I want, the basic idea never leaves me. It rises, grows upward, and I hear and see the picture as a whole take shape and stand forth before me, as though cast in a single piece, so that all that is left is the work of writing it down. This goes quickly, according as I have the time, for sometimes I have several compositions in labour at once, though I am sure never to confuse one with the other.
>
> You will ask me when I take my ideas. That I cannot say with any degree of certainty: they come to me uninvited, directly or indirectly. I could almost grasp them in my hands, out in Nature's

open, in the woods, during my promenades, in the silence of the night, at the earliest dawn. They are roused by moods – which in the poet's case are transmitted into words, and in mine into tones – that sound, roar and storm until at last they take shape for me as notes.[50]

Productivity

Beethoven's sketchbooks show the fertility of his invention: his published works contain only a fraction of his total musical output.

Although absent-minded in many aspects of practical life, Beethoven's daily routine for composing was highly organised. He rose early (like many other creative people). He then made a pot of coffee, having ground a precise number of coffee beans. He worked at his desk throughout the morning and early afternoon. At two or three o'clock, he had a meal. If the weather was good enough, he would usually go for two or three excursions during the morning. From time to time he would pause in order to sketch passages of music. Especially when he was composing, Beethoven was a man of enormous vitality:

> I only live in my music ... I am often engaged on three or four works at the same time.

> Letter to Franz Wegeler, 29 vi 1800[51]

---

[50] Reminiscences of a meeting in Vienna in 1823, written up in 1885, in O. G. Sonneck (ed.), *Beethoven: Impressions by his Contemporaries* (New York: Dover, 1926), pp. 146-147.

[51] A. C. Kalischer (ed.), *The Letters of Ludwig van Beethoven* (London: J. M. Dent, 1909).

Ferdinand Ries, a friend and pupil recalled:

> Beethoven composed part of the second March
> [Op. 45] while – this still seems unbelievable to me
> – giving me a lesson on a sonata which I was due
> to perform that evening.[52]

Character

That Beethoven had a mind and body of rare power was immediately apparent to everyone who met him. For example, the force of Beethoven's personality impressed Liszt (then about 11) when he was taken (by his teacher, Czerny) to meet Beethoven. Despite his own later fame, Liszt said that this meeting with Beethoven 'has remained the greatest pride of my life'.[53]

Karl Johann Braun von Braunthal, a friend of Schubert, was in a restaurant when Beethoven entered:

> A man of middle height, very solidly built, with
> the head of a lion surrounded by a grey mane;
> bright piercing eyes that wandered in all directions.
> [At times] he wandered about uncertainly, as if in a
> dream. When spoken to – or, as more often
> happened, when he was shouted at – by a friend,
> he lifted his eyelids, like an eagle roused from
> slumber.[54]

Friends or strangers often saw Beethoven sitting for hours in a restaurant, consumed by his thoughts and working inwardly on a current composition. At last he would leave the

---

[52] F. Wegeler and F. Ries, *Remembering Beethoven: The Biographical Notes of Franz Wegeler and Ferdinand Ries* (Great Ocean, 1987).

[53] *Beethoven: Impressions by his Contemporaries*, p. 162.

[54] Karl Johann Braun von Braunthal, 'Recollections' (1840).

table (his only 'companion' on some evenings), and offer to pay for a meal which had long since gone cold and which he had therefore not even begun to eat. On other occasions, understanding restauranteurs would forgive their most famous customer when they saw his deserted table and realised that the absent-minded composer (who this time had enjoyed his meal) had wandered out into the street without paying.

Sir Julius Benedict (a conductor and composer, born in Stuttgart) wrote as follows, pointing up the complexity of genius:

> There was in those small piercing eyes an expression which no painter could render. It conveyed a feeling of sublimity and melancholy combined.[55]

A few years ago, a group of scholars were puzzled. They came across several of Beethoven's autograph scores, each of which had a large round mark, like a burn mark. One morning, one of these scholars ran exulting into the archive room. He had been reading the journal of a friend of Beethoven: apparently, Beethoven often used the nearest available manuscript page as a temporary cover to keep his bowl of soup warm.

This story dashed my romantic notions of the great composer, listening to his muse, and writing at such a peak of inspiration that he would be oblivious to the world around him and neglectful of personal and bodily needs. But at last I realised, or conceded, that even Titans have to eat.

What follows is an anecdote from the recollections (1838) of Ferdinand Ries:

> Beethoven was at times extremely short-tempered. One day we were eating lunch in the Swan Inn,

---

[55] Thayer, *The Life of Ludwig Van Beethoven*, pp. 138-140.

and the waiter brought him the wrong dish. No sooner had Beethoven remarked about it – and received an answer from the waiter which was not exactly deferential – then he took the dish (it was so-called Lungenbratel, a roast with plenty of gravy) and flung it at the waiter's head. The poor man carried a large number of plates piled with food on his arm (the Viennese waiters are extremely clever at that), so he was quite helpless. The gravy ran down his face. He and Beethoven shouted and abused each other, while all the other guests laughed loudly. Finally, Beethoven broke off and burst out laughing also at the sight of the waiter with gravy dripping down his face, licking it up with his tongue, trying to curse but forced to resume licking up the gravy and pulling the most ludicrous faces. A picture worthy of a Hogarth.[56]

Deafness

Many are the theories, and long and learned is the speculation, about Beethoven's deafness. But almost 200 years of diligent scholarship have produced no definitive answers to two central questions: 'When did Beethoven first notice signs of dysfunction? And second, what was the cause?'

The first symptom was tinnitus, in itself a source of distress for an already sensitive and self-conscious man. In other words, Beethoven's hurt was manifest in both his social and his musical life. Given that the onset was subtle (and insidious), we can only date the onset of tinnitus to the late 1790s, when he was still in his late twenties.

The year of origin is likely to have been 1796 or 1797. Some twentieth-century doctors, having reviewed the medical evidence, contended that typhus (endemic in Vienna at that

---

[56] *Ibid.*, part II.

time) was the probable cause. But Sir George Grove, in his article on Beethoven for the first edition (1879) of his *Dictionary of Music and Musicians*, concluded that Beethoven's deafness was the result of syphilis, contracted in early adulthood.

We can now be almost 100% sure of the diagnosis, namely that Beethoven suffered from otosclerosis of the mixed type – that is, degeneration of the auditory nerve as well as formation of spongy bone.

After trying every possible form of remedy, from the orthodox to the esoteric, Beethoven reluctantly accepted that the loss of hearing was progressive and incurable. For years, he put up with the indignity of having to use an ear trumpet.

By 1818, Beethoven was completely deaf, and so he could only converse by use of pencil and paper. He had, of course, long before been forced to abandon his career as a pianist (and skilled improviser at the keyboard).

The sadness of his plight was most poignant at a concert when the then-deaf composer rose to applaud the performance of one of his own works, and then found himself gesticulated at (by distant members of the audience who had not recognised him) to shut up and sit down, because the piece of music had not yet reached its conclusion.

Isolation and inspiration

Research studies tell us that (actual or perceived) difference from a group provokes scorn, rejection or bullying – or all three. Why might the young Beethoven have been a victim of this syndrome? First, we have evidence to suggest that his mother may have neglected to ensure that each morning he left home tidy and well turned out. Second, because of his often surly take-it-or-leave-it manner. Third, because his life focus – from early boyhood – was on music. There were the usual pranks between the three brothers, but how often must Ludwig's neighbours and schoolmates have muttered among themselves, 'Why won't Ludwig come out and play with us?

He's always stuck indoors.' Of his school fellows who in after-years wrote their reminiscences of him, not one speaks of him as a playfellow. None has anecdotes to relate games with him, or rambles on the hills, or adventures upon the Rhine or its shores, in which he joined.

A neighbour, Cäcilia Fischer, confirms this:

> One could not say that Ludwig cared much for companions or society ... His happiest hours were those when he was free of all company, when his parents were out, and he was left alone by himself.[57]

The young Ludwig was described by Dr W. C. Müller as 'a shy and taciturn boy – the necessary consequence of leading a life apart – observing and pondering more than speaking, and disposed to abandon himself entirely to the feelings awakened by music and (later) by poetry, and to the pictures created by imagination'.[58] In his adult life, nature and walking gave comfort, and poetry brought solace.

Discord between his parents and teaching pressure from his father left Ludwig disconsolate. Moreover, he was, from early on, nonconformist in accent, clothing, general appearance, manners and behaviour. Despite this catalogue of seemingly insurmountable drawbacks, he did cultivate a gift of friendship. By his early twenties he had formed quite a large circle of friends, many of whom were from Bonn's most respected and discerning families.

As we have seen, from boyhood, Beethoven indulged his desire for solitude. Indeed, one of his friends even coined a word for this tendency, or talent to be self-absorbed. Hélène von Breuning, a young widow, was for a time a second mother to Beethoven. When he was composing or contemplating, she

---

[57] Quoted in Elliot Forbes (ed.), *Thayer's Life of Beethoven*, vol. I (Princeton: Princeton University Press, 1967), p. 59.
[58] *Ibid.*, p. 59.

kept would-be visitors at a discreet distance by whispering, 'Ludwig has his *raptus* again.'[59]

Beethoven was most fully himself in those carefree hours of *raptus*, but we can scarcely imagine how awkward the transition was – for Beethoven, for his friends and for the devoted Frau von Breuning – when he emerged, or tried to emerge into the pale light of everyday life.

J. L. Blahtka,[60] writing in 1840 to Anton Schindler,[61] one of Beethoven's biographers, recalled Beethoven as a man who 'being confined to his own world of ideas, had never learned to step out of himself'.[62]

Beethoven's increasing deafness was the most severe embarrassment, both personally and professionally:

> I must confess that I am living a miserable life. For almost two years, I have ceased to attend any social functions, just because I find it impossible to say to people 'I am deaf'. If I had any other profession, it would be easier; but in mine it is a terrible handicap. As for my enemies – of whom I have a fair number – what would they say?[63]

> You can scarcely imagine what a dreary, sad life I have been leading during the past couple of years. My weak hearing seemed always to be haunting me, and I ran away from people, was forced to

---

[59] *Ibid.,* p. 108.

[60] Father of a pianist; a torchbearer at Beethoven's funeral.

[61] For several years he was Beethoven's unpaid secretary, factotum and agent. His biography, though useful, is not wholly reliable. During the composer's life, Schindler conducted all nine symphonies.

[62] A. C. Kalischer (ed.), *The Letters of Ludwig van Beethoven* (London: J. M. Dent, 1909).

[63] Letter to Dr Franz Gerhard Wegeler, 29 vi 1800 in *Ibid.*

appear a misanthrope, though not all in my character.[64]

For the rest of his life, Beethoven had to draw on all his powers of resilience and endurance:

I have often cursed my existence. Plutarch taught me stoicism. If nothing is possible, I will defy my fate.[65]

There is yet one more factor which led to Beethoven's quasi-separation from the world: the apartness of genius, the loneliness of being a pioneer – in any field of human endeavour. Alfred Einstein expands on this theme:

The inevitability of the great is caused by the task to which they are committed; and the urge to accomplish that task to the utmost degree ...

Every great artist is both happy and unhappy. He knows the joy of creating, to which no other bliss on earth can be compared. Yet every great artist is unhappy too. He feels a resistance to the world; and a resistance in and from the world – its slowness to comprehend.[66]

Beethoven's journals are full of words of encouragement to himself:

The chief characteristic of a distinguished man: endurance in harsh circumstances.[67]

---

[64] Letter to Wegeler, 16 xi 1801, in *Ibid.*
[65] Letter to Wegeler, 29 iv 1800 in *Ibid.*
[66] Alfred Einstein, *Greatness in Music* (Oxford: Oxford University Press, 1945), p. 164.
[67] No. 93.

Here I quote from Einstein again:

> Greatness means the construction of an inner world, and the communication of the inner world to all humanity. ...
>
> An inner world does not come into being without struggle, without search and resistance.[68]

That last sentence is close to what Jung wrote about the way of individuation. In Jung's formulation, deep personal growth is stimulated by enduring – and learning from – doubt, delay and disappointment, as well as a fundamental reappraisal of one's roots and early conditioning.

Beethoven's isolation gave him more time and inner space for composing.

Two factors forced Beethoven to turn ever-more inwards. First, the diminishing prospect that he would ever marry; second, he was denied (by progressive loss of hearing) the parallel career of the virtuoso pianist, touring the capitals of Europe. Moreover, Beethoven was well equipped to make the most fruitful use of those added hours of solitude, because of his physical stamina, his powers of concentration and his total dedication to music.

The Heiligenstadt Testament

In the autumn of 1822, when he was almost 32, Beethoven was staying at Heiligenstadt, a village outside Vienna. While he was there he wrote the most famous document in the history of music, since known as the Heiligenstadt Testament. This very personal statement was written for his brothers, and was not discovered until after his death. The manuscript is very carefully written, with few erasures or corrections, as proof of

---

[68] Einstein, *Greatness in Music*, p. 164.

the attention he gave to the first draft before the final copy was made. Here are two core sentences:

> I must live as an exile.
> I would have put an end to my life: only art withheld me.[69]

Despite (or growing beyond) such near-suicidal despair, he was able to return to Vienna with the Second Symphony, and he entered a new phase of enhanced creativity (his middle period), characterised by the heroic tone of his only opera, *Fidelio* (libretto and music in praise of freedom). The unmistakable hallmark of triumph, after difficulty is overcome, is evident in the 'Eroica' Symphony (1803-04), and of course in the Fifth Symphony, sometimes nicknamed (though not by Beethoven) 'Fate Knocks at the Door'.

We have no parallel, in the history of music, of any other composer of the first rank losing his hearing at such a young age. The blow was all the harder because the hearing was hitherto so keen and delicate, especially to birdsong during his country walks. But the cruelty of the blow (to self-esteem, to social life and to his secondary career as pianist and conductor) is more than matched by the glory of his response. From Heiligenstadt onwards – right through to the visionary quality of the late quartets – the music Beethoven composed is raised to a new dimension – and from an already high base. His technique is freer, musical invention is perfectly wedded to form, and the artistic–human drama is both touching and trenchant (as in the Violin Concerto). It is as though he shook his fist at fate, and shouted in defiance, 'I will show myself complete master of my art.'

About a year before Heiligenstadt, Beethoven wrote to his best friend, Dr Franz Wegeler:

---

[69] Beethoven, Heiligenstadt Testament, 6 x, 1802. Available at:
http://www.beethoven.ws/heiligenstadt_testament.html (accessed 20th April 2017).

O that I could be free from it [the evil of my weakening hearing], and encompass the world! ...

Every day I approach nearer to the goal: this I feel, though I can scarcely describe it. Only through this can your Beethoven live. Don't talk [to me] of rest! ...

I shall seize fate by the throat: it will certainly never wholly overcome me. Oh! Life is so beautiful. Would that I could have a thousand lives![70]

This letter shows not the grandiosity of delusion, but the ambition of genius. He did fulfil this ambition: his music and his name do (and will always) 'encompass the world'.

I am not for one moment suggesting that Heiligenstadt led to a resurrection of Beethoven's spirits – nothing so dramatic or mystical. Beethoven did, indeed, from 1802–03 experience an enlivening of the artistic libido. But this was a breakthrough waiting to happen. After all, the progressive loss of hearing was the most severe, but not the first, crisis. And, from early boyhood, there was year after year of constant musical input and output. In addition, Beethoven had the advantage of his general good health. Every doctor who examined him marvelled at the strong torso and assured him that his condition was robust. Heiligenstadt, therefore, is best seen as a trigger or catalyst.

He seized his moment. His will to succeed is an example to all of us. And his creative life is a supreme example of the way nature compensates – in Beethoven's case, over-compensates – for weakness or deprivation.

In his twenties, Beethoven admired the ideals of the French Revolution. But his number one hero was Brutus, that hater of tyranny – a political idealist who was not very adept at reading or anticipating the wiles of enemies, current or potential.

---

[70] Wegeler and Ries, *Remembering Beethoven*, Letter 16 xi 1801.

The central message of Heiligenstadt is that the way to triumph over adversity is to increase one's love of humanity. In doing so, Beethoven established himself as a hero in the world of music. Just as important, he became a hero to himself.

Beethoven's Violin Concerto

1806 was a golden year for Beethoven. In that year he sketched and completed his Violin Concerto. As if this one masterpiece were not achievement enough, within a 12-month period he also completed the Fourth Piano Concerto, the 'Appassionata' sonata, and the three quartets (Op. 59) dedicated to the Russian Ambassador in Vienna, Count Andreas Razumovsky, a fine amateur violinist. And there is even more in the musical legacy (or litany) of 1806: he wrote the Third Leonora Overture and the Fourth Symphony, and composed a substantial part of the Fifth Symphony. Beethoven was now master of the world of music. He was only 36.

On the manuscript score of the Violin Concerto, Beethoven made a pun in his inscription: he begs the clemency of its first performer, Clement. Franz Clement was a Viennese violinist, conductor and composer. He was a violinist in the Vienna Imperial Opera House Orchestra from the age of nine. In London, two years later, he played concertos under the baton of Haydn. At the age of 14, he received an admiring letter from Beethoven, who had recently heard the young boy perform.

As an adult, too, Clement was held in high regard by Beethoven. Not only was Clement given the honour of conducting the first performance of the 'Eroica' Symphony (April 1805), but he also had many editorial sessions with Beethoven during the composition of the Violin Concerto.

Although Beethoven had studied the violin in his youth, and had an insider's understanding of the character of the instrument, he was first and foremost a pianist. The autograph score assigns four staves to the solo part, in order to make space for alterations. In many places, all four staves have been filled – a clear indication of the value and number of Clement's suggestions.

The first performance was given in Vienna on 23 December 1806, with Clement as soloist. Because of the length of the concerto, the first movement took up the whole of the first half of the concert; the slow movement and the finale were played after the interval.

During the interval, Clement gave the audience a circus turn. He performed one of his own sonatas, played on one string only, and with the violin held upside down!

But the main enterprise of the evening was far removed from fun and acrobatics. Every member of the orchestra was tense. Beethoven himself was nervous, not about the worth of the new work, but wondering if, without a single rehearsal, the orchestral players' sight-reading would do him and his new concerto justice.

As was often the case, Beethoven completed the work only just in time. The mass of crossings-out show that he was rewriting until just before the concert. Nonetheless, he was justifiably confident about his soloist. Clement had a phenomenal memory for music, and all his work with Beethoven during the weeks of composition made up for the lack of time to practise the final version.

I feel ashamed to include a story against a fellow music critic; but this is what a not-so-bright reviewer reported on 8th January 1807, in Vienna's *Journal for Drama, Music and Poetry*:

> The verdict of the *cognoscenti* is unanimous. They conceded that this concerto has some beauty, but maintain that the continuity is often completely fragmented, and that the endless repetition of commonplace passages soon becomes wearisome. They assert that Beethoven could put his undoubtedly great talent to better use.

This work is far longer – and more intricate – than any previous violin concerto. Although there are bravura passages – for a virtuoso to show their skill – Beethoven did not write merely for effect: we find no display for the sake of display. The shortest interval has its own meaning and place in the architecture of the music. Always Beethoven's intention is artistic, not rhetorical. The most delicate harmonic allusion is eloquent. There are many original touches in all three movements.

The design is so spacious, the proportions classically perfect, and the melodic invention so rich, so unfailingly beautiful, that I still find it hard to believe what Beethoven's friend and pupil, Carl Czerny, assures us: that the concerto was finished only hours – at most, a day or two – before the first performance. But, as we have seen, the autograph score shows many last-minute changes and improvements. Beethoven was a compulsive reviser – and with what results!

The prevailing mood of Beethoven's Violin Concerto is serenity. Even during the jaunty, village-inn atmosphere of the finale, Beethoven's emphasis is on the lyrical, songlike quality of the violin. The first subject of the first movement is a radiant, chorale-like theme, announced *dolce* by the woodwind. This establishes the tonality of D major, and sets the tone for the rest of the work. But note two exceptions: the G minor episode in the development section of the first movement, and the G minor episode in the finale.

In these two episodes, Milstein's playing gives us depth of feeling, without maudlin sentiment. He was a naturalised American, born in Odessa. His expression of pathos was a revelation of Beethoven's genius. I suggest that Milstein found inspiration from wounds-to-the-heart in the Russian collective unconscious. And Milstein's lively temperament gave him a special affinity for the music of Beethoven.

In music, tension is expressed in two main ways: the tension of contrast, and the tension of waiting. Unlike the other concerto from this same year, the Fourth Piano Concerto (in which the soloist makes their entry in the first bar), Beethoven here reverts to the usual classical-period formula – an opening orchestral *tutti*.

This *tutti* is both strong and long – so long, indeed, that in the concert hall one can sense mounting excitement in the audience, enjoying the grand procession of themes but impatient to hear the voice of the solo violin. We hold our breath, waiting to hear if the violinist can meet the technical demands of those majestic opening octaves, steeply ascending, climbing to a high held G.

In his autobiography Milstein says:

> One of my favourite revelations is the cadenza in the first movement, in which Beethoven varies the main theme in such a way that the listener is kept waiting for its return with increasing tension. And, when it does reappear, it is like heavenly song.[71]

The second type of tension is the tension of contrast. Furtwängler states, 'Music is not a sequence of notes, but a struggle of forces.'[72] What is true in the arts is also true in human beings: a person who is psychologically and emotionally mature has reconciled (or, to be more specific, is constantly blending) opposites in personality and background (or upbringing). Thus, our Lord was both gentle and strong. He was far-seeing and also fully open to this person, this place, this living moment. Jesus was (and is) endearing in humanity, enduring (and glorious) in His divinity.

The opening pages of Beethoven's Violin Concerto are among the most splendid (and the most statuesque) in all music. Here we have a study in contrasts. The concerto opens with five drum taps – five evenly played repetitions of the same

---

[71] Nathan Milstein, trans. Antonina Bouis, *From Russia to the West* (New York: Proscenium Publishers, 1990).

[72] Wilhelm Furtwängler, *Notebooks 1924–1954* (Quartet Books, 1989), Entry for 1946.

note. The marking is *piano*, but the atmosphere is menacing, even fateful. This introduces woodwind – oboes, clarinets and bassoons. Only a poet can achieve so natural a dialogue – between drum and woodwind, martial drama and pastoral song, danger and safety. The Roman school of painters had a definition of beauty that applies also to music, especially of the classical period: their maxim was 'multitude in unity'.

A great piece of music has this paradox: it combines the maximum of power with the maximum of delicacy. Of no masterwork is this more true than Beethoven's Violin Concerto.

Greatness in music

Four years before he wrote his Violin Concerto, Beethoven knew he would eventually become completely deaf. He was only 32. The malady was incurable. So this concerto – like all his subsequent works, notably the last quartets – is in one sense a triumph of art over weakness and adversity. In another sense his composition is informed and enhanced by weakness and adversity.

For an artist – as well as for a patient in psychotherapy – suffering is not an experience to avoid or run away from. Rather it is an emotion to be faced and worked with. To a patient, suffering is the raw material (in both senses) of personal growth. To a composer, poet or painter, suffering is both a spur to creativity and an invaluable source or wellspring for a sonata, poem or painting.[73] If Beethoven's hearing had

---

[73] Monet provides another interesting example of courage and dedication in producing truly original great art despite (or because of) a major deterioration of his first faculty. In 1908 – with 18 years of productive life still remaining – his eyesight began to fail. He suffered from blurred vision, cataracts in both eyes and difficulty in identifying colours. His magnificent water lilies series is characterised by vigorous brushwork, freedom (such as in the dissolving images) and less painting over than before. Had Monet's eyesight stayed

remained normal, would we have had the mysterious deeps of the late quartets?

Beethoven's Violin Concerto is integrated, organic. The music is substantial because *he* was substantial. He was broken, yet whole. Beethoven was isolated socially, but his true community was the whole musical world. This vision gave Beethoven his artistic strength and stature. This vision gave Beethoven his endurance, his will to live.

Furtwängler said, 'The meaning of art always consists in moving from the individual to the general'.[74] Why does Beethoven's Violin Concerto have universal outreach? Why is it music for all time? Here is Furtwängler again, defining for us the central criterion of greatness in music, or in any of the fine arts:

> The crucial question is always: Is the art-work ornamental and decorative, or does it grasp life? Does it reflect the whole of life?[75]

A great work of art has five characteristics:

- We identify with its message and its emotions.

- It leads to self-knowledge, self-discovery.

- It enters the soul.

- It wins a permanent place in our memory, our imagination, our aesthetic (or personal culture), our way of seeing life.

- It enables the soul and the senses to be more alert during future occasions of potential heightened experience.

---

relatively unimpaired, would he have produced so many original touches late in his long career?
[74] *Notebook* 1924.
[75] *Ibid.*, p. 93.

When we listen to Beethoven's Violin Concerto, we sense –
we are sure – that this composer is authentic. Nothing is for
show. He himself is a true original, and so he does not need to
raise his voice or strain for novelty.

The newness arose from deep artistic impulse, and so the
music transcends fashion or period. It will always live. It will
always speak. It will give hope to each generation.

Nothing is contrived in Beethoven's Violin Concerto: we
know he is composing from first-hand contact. In this work,
every melody, every single bar has been experienced. This is
real life, not theory or doctrine. Beethoven gives us his
humanity; he gives us his nobility. The music is personal, even
intimate; it is also – especially in the repose of the *larghetto* –
universal and timeless.

> Greatness without warmth is empty. In his Violin
> Concerto, Beethoven attained equilibrium: an ideal
> synthesis of the musical and the spiritual.[76]

---

[76] *Ibid., Notebook* 1939.

Listening

Listening to music is a model or paradigm for all forms of listening – to birdsong, to the rustle of leaves, to the human voice, to one's inner voice, and – most importantly – to the will of God. To develop your skills in one form of listening can enhance all forms of listening. The greater the work, the greater the task of the musicians (conductor, soloist and orchestra) – and the greater the task of the audience:

> A work of art is a king: one must wait to be addressed by it. One must take trouble over it; one must take time. It does not want to be considered, tasted, felt; but, rather, absorbed in its entirety, by the whole person. That requires strength and time.[77]

What, in detail, should we listen for while Milstein plays Beethoven's Violin Concerto? I invite you to delight in:

- The long, seamless line, and the consistency of the interpretation of the whole work

- The agility of bowing and fingering

- The passionate climaxes

- The delicate, multi-hued vibrato

- The intonation always middle of the note

---

[77] *Ibid., Notebook* 1939.

- The top notes, pure yet vibrant

Here is how Furtwängler suggests a great work should be played:

> Treat a masterpiece, not in its dried condition, but as a living plant – resplendent in its natural colours – allowing it to grow and unfold in front of the audience.[78]

People who knew Milstein considered him to be a straight-talking, feet-on-the-ground person. So when he uses religious language, we sit up and take special note. In his autobiography, he described Beethoven's Violin Concerto as 'a miracle ... like a divine message'.[79] He was in no doubt about the size of the challenge. The recording I invite you to listen to as you end this book is that of Milstein playing with the Pittsburgh Symphony Orchestra under William Steinberg – which was made in January 1955. Milstein was 51. As you will soon hear for yourself, he was then at the height of his powers, artistic and technical. The first and third movement cadenzas are Milstein's own.

Finale

Jung suggested that the bigger the person, the bigger the shadow side: this large shadow is partly created by the behaviour and the unconscious drives of the person themselves; in part, the shadow is formed by the projections and the (often over-stated) expectations of their family, acolytes and envious competitors.

---

[78] *Ibid., Notebook* 1939.
[79] *From Russia to the West*, p. 91.

If we expand Jung's insight, we can say that the bigger the person, the more and the bigger are the paradoxes in their life and work. In 1802 Beethoven came near to suicide. In 1806 he composed the Violin Concerto, the Fourth Piano Concerto, the Fourth Symphony and most of the Fifth Symphony. In only four years, he made the journey from despair to musical glory.

> In his life, the highest assurance of realisation is blended with the most cruel ordeal or denial.

Heinrich Friedrich Rellstab (a writer), 1825

A second paradox is that he was an isolated man who saw himself as a social outcast. Beethoven was notoriously careless about his clothes and general appearance. Indeed, he was once questioned in the street by police on suspicion of being a tramp. Now he has a permanent place in the hearts and minds of each new generation.

The writing – for both soloist and orchestra – establishes this Violin Concerto as one of the finest works of Western art. It is right at the top, along with the best of Rodin, Rembrandt and Michelangelo.

At this level of influence – restricting this concerto, for a moment, to the realms of music – Beethoven is a bringer of joy and beauty. But this work is more than great art: it is a triumph of the human spirit, written by an almost deaf composer. At this enhanced level of influence, Beethoven's Violin Concerto is a source not only of joy and beauty, but also of hope and strength for all time.

In part of his psyche, Beethoven was dejected – a proud man humbled. But he transmuted human sorrow into spiritual utterance. I use the word 'spiritual' advisedly. I cannot account for my awe – when I hear (or think about or read a score of) this concerto – in rational or psychological or musical technical terms. I do believe that Beethoven had access to the divine. I have an ally in the art critic Peter Fuller. He has warned us that we are losing the concept of art as a channel of grace.

In the previous section, I outlined five criteria which must be met before one can regard a work of art as truly great. I now find it necessary to add one more factor: the sixth in our list, but surely – in order of importance – the first:

Great art reminds us of our divine origin.

Furtwängler[80]

For Beethoven's own view about the sources of his inspiration, we have the recollections of Johann Andreas Stumpff, a maker of musical instruments. He quotes verbatim what Beethoven said while seated on a grassy mound on a lovely autumn day:

> Here surrounded by the products of Nature, I often sit for hours, while my senses feast upon the spectacle of the conceiving and multiplying children of nature ... Here the blue sky is my sublime roof.
>
> When in the evening, I contemplate the sky in wonder, and the host of luminous bodies ... my spirit rises beyond these constellations, so many millions of miles away, to the primal source – from which all creation flows, and from which new creations will flow eternally ... Yes, that which excites the heart must come from above: otherwise the music is nothing but notes: body without spirit. Of what value is body without spirit?
>
> The spirit must rise from the earth, in which for a time the divine spark is confined. Much like

---

[80] *Notebook*, 1939.

the field to which the ploughman entrusts precious seed, the human spirit must flower and bear much fruit; and, thus multiplied, rise again towards the source from which it has flown. For only by persistent toil of the faculties granted to us do we created beings serve and revere the creator and preserver of infinite nature.

Baden (Beethoven's usual summer habitat), late September 1824

Beethoven was not religious in the conventional churchgoing sense. But even St Francis himself (the archetypal lover of nature) would surely be justifiably pleased to fashion such a felicitous Sermon on the Grassy Mound.

Beethoven's principal illness, at the end of his life, was a liver disease, combined with dropsy; his heart remained strong. He died during a thunderstorm on 26th March 1827, aged 56. Three days later, beside the grave, Grillparzer's[81] funeral oration was delivered by Heinrich Anschütz, one of Vienna's leading actors. Here are two extracts:

To be sure, the hero of German melodious poetry [Goethe] still lives, and long may he live! But the master of tuneful song – the heir and amplifier of the immortal fame of Handel and Bach, of Haydn and Mozart – has expired; and we weep as we stand by the broken strings of the silent harp ...

Return home, grieving but composed. And if ever the force of his creations overwhelms you like an onrushing tempest – when your ecstasy overflows amid a generation as yet unborn – then remember this hour, and think; we were there

[81] Grillparzer (then 36) had known Beethoven since about 1805. Anschütz had also known Beethoven, though less well than Grillparzer did.

when they buried him; and when he died, we wept.[82]

The saga of Beethoven's life is twofold, musical and personal. One is the musical development from Heiligenstadt, in 1802, through to the Ode to Joy at the end of the Ninth Symphony (composed 1822–24). Those 20 creative years were also the journey of a soul. In any hour of doubt or difficulty, we can all be inspired by the courage of a brave man.

Beethoven surely knew – even if he never articulated it thus – that God gives us music so that we can also praise Him without words.

Coda

The giving of oneself to a piece of music (or to a person), in total openness, is an archetypal experience. It eludes description. It is something we do – or aspire to do. In this state of integrity (and relaxed intensity), we grow in love. Love invites us to transcend our previously assumed limitations.

> All great art is the work of the whole living creature, body and soul, and chiefly of the soul. But it is not only the work of the whole creature, it likewise addresses the whole creature. That in which the perfect being speaks must also have the perfect being to listen. I am not to spend my utmost spirit, and give all my strength and life to my work, while you, spectator or hearer, will give me only the attention of half your soul. You must be all mine, as I am all yours; it is the only condition on which we can meet each other. All your faculties, all that is in you of greatest and best, must be awake in you, or I have no reward.

---

[82] *Beethoven: Impressions by his Contemporaries*, p. 229.

The painter is not to cast the entire treasure of his human nature into his labour merely to lease a part of the beholder: not merely to beguile him into emotion, not merely to lead him into thought; but to do all this. Senses, fancy, feeling, reason, the whole of the beholding spirit, must be stilled in attention or stirred with delight.[83]

'O music, where speech ends, your speech begins.' That quotation by Rilke is my cue to move aside: Milstein is ready to play for us.

Surrender yourself. Give yourself totally to the experience. Be not only a listener, but also a participant. Be alert, as if this is your first hearing of the work.

People of prayer know what it is to become one with God. Now let us – each of us – be one with Beethoven's Violin Concerto – and through it draw nearer to the heartbeat of God.

Mine ear is open and my heart prepar'd.

Shakespeare, *Richard II*, III ii

---

[83] John Ruskin, *The Stones of Venice*, volume III (London: George Allen, 1925).

Select Bibliography

Barclay, Robert, *An Apology for the True Christian Divinity* (London: T. Sowle Raylton & Luke Hinde, 1736).

Beethoven, Ludwig van, Heiligenstadt Testament, 6 x, 1802. (http://www.beethoven.ws/heiligenstadt_testament.html) (accessed 20th April 2017).

Bion, Wilfred, 'Notes on Memory and Desire', *The Psycho-analytic Forum*, 1967, Vol. 2, No. 3.

Bloom, Anthony, *School of Prayer* (London: Darton, Longman and Todd, 1993).

De Sales, St Francis, trans. Elisabeth Stopp, *St Francis de Sales, Selected Letters* (London: Faber and Faber, 1960).

Durrell, Lawrence, *Bitter Lemons in Cyprus* (London: Faber and Faber, 2000).

Einstein, Alfred, *Greatness in Music* (Oxford: Oxford University Press, 1945).

Elchaninov, Alexander, *The Diary of a Russian Priest* (St Vladimir's Seminary, 1997).

Epictetus, trans. Robert Dobbin, *Discourses and Selected Writings* (London: Penguin, 2008).

Forsyth, P. T., ed. Jason A. Goroncy, *Descending on Humanity and Intervening in History: Notes from the Pulpit* (Oregon: Pickwick, 2013).

Francis de Sales, St, ed. Sisters of the Visitation, *St Francis de Sales in his Letters* (London: Sands & Co, 1954).

Freud, Sigmund, *Five Lectures on Psycho-Analysis* (London: Penguin, 1995).

Furlong, Monica, *With Love to the Church* (London: Hodder and Stoughton, 1965).

Furtwängler, Wilhelm, *Notebooks 1924–1954* (Quartet Books, 1989).

Hammarskjöld, Dag, trans. W. H. Auden and Leif Sjöberg, *Markings* (London: Faber and Faber, 1964).

Heraclitus, trans. G. S. Clark, *The Cosmic Fragments* (Cambridge: Cambridge University Press, 1954).

Huxley, Aldous, *The Art of Seeing* (London: Chatto and Windus, 1964).

Ignatius of Loyola, St, trans. Anthony Mottola, *The Spiritual Exercises of St Ignatius* (New York: Doubleday, 1989).

Illich, Ivan, 'The Eloquence of Silence' in *Celebration of Awareness* (London: Marion Boyars, 1971).

Jones, Ernest, *The Life and Works of Sigmund Freud* (London: Penguin 1964).

Jung, Carl Gustav, *Memories, Dreams and Reflections* (London: Fontana Press, 1995).

Jung, Carl Gustav, *Modern Man in Search of a Soul* (London: Routledge Classics, 2001).

Kalischer, A., ed., *The Letters of Ludwig van Beethoven* (London: J. M. Dent, 1909).

Klein, Melanie, 'Our Adult World and Its Roots in Infancy' in *Envy and Gratitude and Other Works 1946–1963* (London: Vintage Press, 1997), pp. 247-264.

Lavater, Johann, *Aphorisms on Man* (London: J. Johnson, 1791).

Maeterlinck, Maurice, trans. Alfred Sutro, 'The Deeper Life' in *The Treasure of the Humble* (London: George Allen, 1897).

Maslow, Abraham, *The Farther Reaches of Human Nature* (New York: Viking, 1971).

Milstein, Nathan, trans. Antonina Bouis, *From Russia to the West* (New York: Proscenium Publishers, 1990).

Nouwen, Henri, *Reaching Out: The Three Movements of the Spiritual Life* (New York: Doubleday, 2000).

Pascal, Blaise, trans. A. J. Krailsheimer, *Pensées* (London: Penguin, 1995).

Penn, William, *Fruits of a Father's Love: Being the Advice of William Penn to his Children* (London: James Phillips, 1793).

Piper, W., Anthony S. Joyce, Mary McCallum and Hassan F. A. Azim, 'Concentration and Correspondence of Transference Interpretations in Short-Term Psychotherapy', *Journal of Consulting and Clinical Psychology* 113, Vol. 61. No 4, pp. 586-595.

Ruskin, John, *The Stones of Venice*, volume III (London: George Allen, 1925).

Sonneck, O. G., ed., *Beethoven: Impressions by his Contemporaries* (New York: Dover, 1926).

Teresa of Ávila, St, trans. A Discalced Carmelite, *The Interior Castle* (London: Sands & Co, 1945).

Thayer, Alexander Wheelock, *The Life of Ludwig Van Beethoven* (New York: General Books, 2009).

Thomas à Kempis, *The Imitation of Christ* (London: Oxford University Press, 1900).

Tillich, Paul, *The New Being* (London: University of Nebraska Press, 1955).

Ward, Benedicta SLG, *The Sayings of the Desert Fathers* (London: Mowbray, 1975).

Wegeler, F. and F. Ries, *Remembering Beethoven: The Biographical Notes of Franz Wegeler and Ferdinand Ries* (Great Ocean, 1987).

Winnicott, Donald W., 'The Capacity to be Alone' (1959) in *The Maturational Processes and the Facilitating Environment* (London: Karnac, 1965).

Yeats, W. B., 'Long-legged Fly' in *The Collected Works of W. B. Yeats: Volume I: The Poems* (New York: Scribner, 1989).